# OXFORD *Primary* GEOGRAPHY

Series Consultant **2** Steve Harrison

**Phil Almond    John Lancaster**
**Lynn Lancaster    Pam Jervis    Cathy Wilson**

# OXFORD

The publishers wish to thank the following for permission to reproduce copyright material:

Doug Armand/Tony Stone p.28 (B); Oliver Benn/Tony Stone p.35; M. and V. Birley/TROPIX p.28 (A and C), p.38; Brighton Reference Library p.19 *bottom left* and *bottom right*; Contour Design p.11; Paul Drummond p.14; Edal Photos p.18, p.20, p.26 (1, 2 and 4); Greg Evans International p.14 *right*; FLPA p.16; The Ford Motor Company p.30; B. Gibbs p.21, p.24; Malcolm Gibson/Tony Stone p.28 (F); Geoff Johnson/Tony Stone p.15 *centre*; John and Lynn Lancaster p.4, p.5, p.6 *bottom right*, p.7, p.8, p.9, p.10; Arif Mahmood/Parvez Khan p.40, p.41, p.42, p.43 *top right, centre right* and *left, bottom left*, p.44, p.45, p.46, p.47; Jon Nicholson/Tony Stone p.16 (C); North Picture Library p.14 *top left*; Ordnance Survey p.11; G. and J. Paine p.26 (3); Bryan Parsley/Tony Stone p.15 *bottom*; Ken Paver p.4 *top*, p.6 *left*; Ed Pritchard/Tony Stone p.16 (A); Rohan/Tony Stone p.13 *bottom right*; Helene Rogers/TRIP p.16 (D); Spanish Office of Tourism p.13 *top right*; Paul Thompson/TRIP p.28 (D); Thought Factory p.6 *top*; TRIP p.15; West Country Tourist Board p.13 *top left*; Adam Woolfitt/Susan Griggs p.13 *bottom left*.

The front cover picture was by Haddon Davies Photography.

Illustrations by: Jane Bottomley, Jane Fern, Peter Lawrence, Shelagh McNicholas, Tony Morris, Alan Rose.

Oxford University Press, Walton Street, Oxford OX2 6DP

*Oxford    New York*
*Athens    Auckland    Bangkok    Bombay*
*Calcutta    Cape Town    Dar es Salaam    Delhi*
*Florence    Hong Kong    Istanbul    Karachi*
*Kuala Lumpar    Madras    Madrid    Melbourne*
*Mexico City    Nairobi    Paris    Singapore*
*Taipei    Tokyo    Toronto*
and associated companies in
*Berlin* and *Ibadan*

# Contents

## Askrigg is a village in the Yorkshire Dales.

Look carefully at these photographs for clues about the village.

*A view of the village*

*Main Street, Askrigg*

**Tasks**

1 Is Askrigg a large settlement or a small settlement?

2 What can you see outside the village?

3 What do you think this land is used for?

4 What materials are the buildings made of?

5 Are the same materials used for the buildings where you live?

6 Would you like to live in Askrigg? Give reasons for your answer.

There are only three shops in Askrigg.
*This gift shop sells books and sweets.*

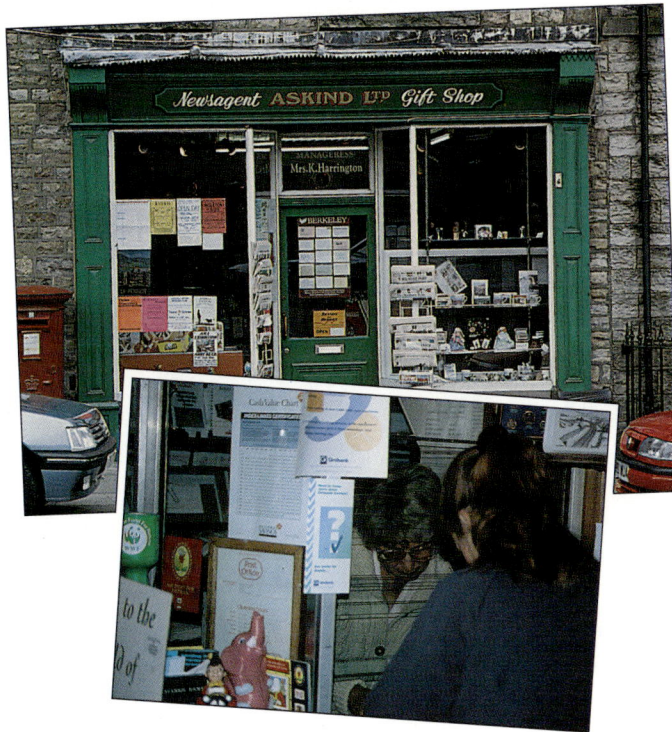

This gift shop is at the edge of the village.

*The Post Office is a small corner of the gift shop.*

*A small supermarket*

**7** Copy and complete the chart.
  a) Tick the items a local person can buy in Askrigg.
  b) Tick the items a local person cannot buy in Askrigg.
  c) Add six items of your own.

**8** Where could local people buy items they cannot find in Askrigg?
  a) In a smaller settlement.
  b) In a larger settlement.

**9** List ten items visitors might buy from the shops.

**10** Compare your locality with Askrigg. Tick the shops in your locality.

**Shopping in Askrigg**

| Item | yes | no |
|---|---|---|
| stamp | | |
| bread | | |
| new bike | | |
| tin of beans | | |
| new pair of shoes | | |
| video player | | |

| Shop | Askrigg | My locality |
|---|---|---|
| Supermarket | ✔ | |
| Post Office | ✔ | |
| Gift Shop | ✔ | |
| Newsagent | | |
| Butchers | | |
| Shoe Shop | | |
| Bakers | | |

## Why do people visit Askrigg?

Askrigg was used in a famous television series called 'All Creatures Great and Small'. Today tourists come to visit the places which were filmed.

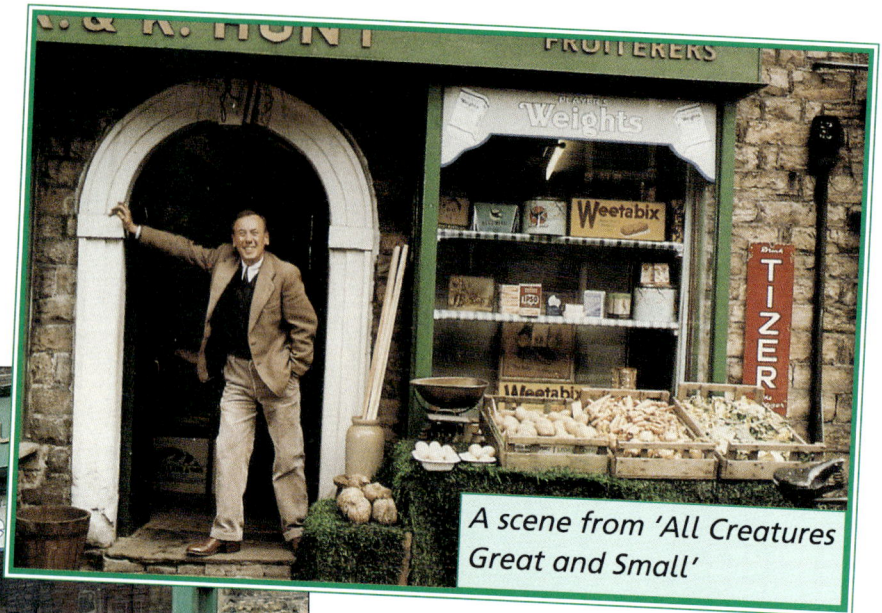

*A scene from 'All Creatures Great and Small'*

*This is what the shop looks like today.*

*A woodturner has opened a workshop on Main Street.*

**Tasks**

1 Look at the photographs on pages 4 to 11 to help you decide why people visit Askrigg. Then copy and complete the chart

2 Think of some reasons of your own.

3 Draw a picture of something you would like to see or do in Askrigg.

| Reasons for visiting Askrigg | Yes | No |
|---|---|---|
| Spend the day shopping | | |
| Go swimming with friends | | |
| Walk in the countryside | | |
| Go down a pothole | | |
| Visit a place they have seen on T.V. | | |
| Have fun in an amusement park | | |
| Look at waterfalls | | |

6

*This is where the railway used to run. Some people want to rebuild it.*

A coach parked in the village centre.

Cars parked on Main Street.

Setting off on a walk.

**Tasks**

4  What problems are caused when a lot of people visit Askrigg?

5  How would a new railway help local people?

6  How would a new railway help tourists?

7  Design a poster to advertise a day trip to Askrigg.

8  Imagine you are visiting Askrigg. Describe what you would do and see when you got there.

9  Draw a picture of something you think might spoil Askrigg.

## Different rocks produce different shaped features.

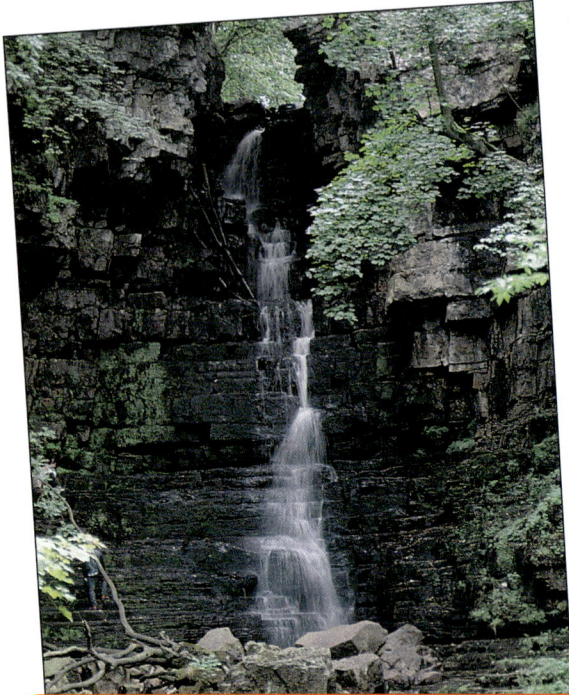

There are three kinds of rock around Askrigg.

**Limestone** is strong but it dissolves in water.

**Sandstone** is quite a hard rock.

**Shale** is a softer rock. Water can cut it away.

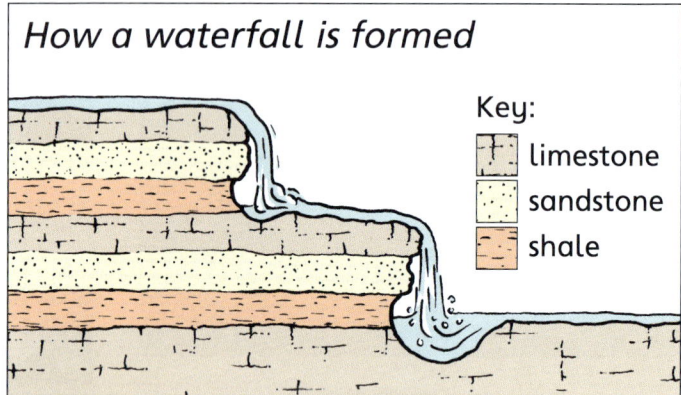

How a waterfall is formed

Key:
- limestone
- sandstone
- shale

**Tasks**

Look at these photographs and drawings of the waterfall.

1 What kind of rock is a) at the top b) at the bottom?

2 Why are there broken trees and branches at the bottom?

3 Describe what is happening to the rock at the bottom of the waterfall.

4 These are potholes near Askrigg. What do you think has made the holes?

5 Why have farmers used stone to build their walls?

6 Where do you think the stone has come from?

7 Make a list of things that you think local people and farmers have used stone for.

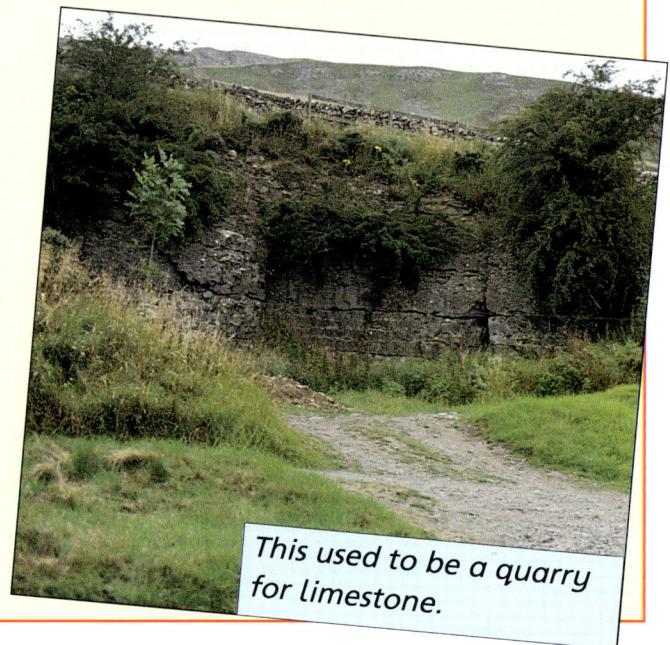

This used to be a quarry for limestone.

# Things that grow in a place give you clues about the land there.

Here you can see a rocky hillside above Askrigg.

*Poppies grow in meadows.*

*Betony grows in limestone soil.*

*'Stinking Bob' grows in limestone places.*

*Lady's Bedstraw grows in grassy soil with a lot of lime.*

*Water Lilies float in ponds.*

*Cowslips are rare in the north.*

**Task**

8  Imagine you are going for a walk up the hill in the picture above. Copy and complete this table to show which flowers you might see.

| Name | Colour | Where it grows | On the walk |
|------|--------|----------------|-------------|
| betony | | limestone soil | |
| | white | | no |
| cowslip | | meadows – not in the north | |
| | pink | | yes |
| | red | in meadows | |
| lady's bedstraw | | soil with lots of lime | |

## What is the area around Askrigg like?

The photographs and maps on these pages show what the area around Askrigg is like.

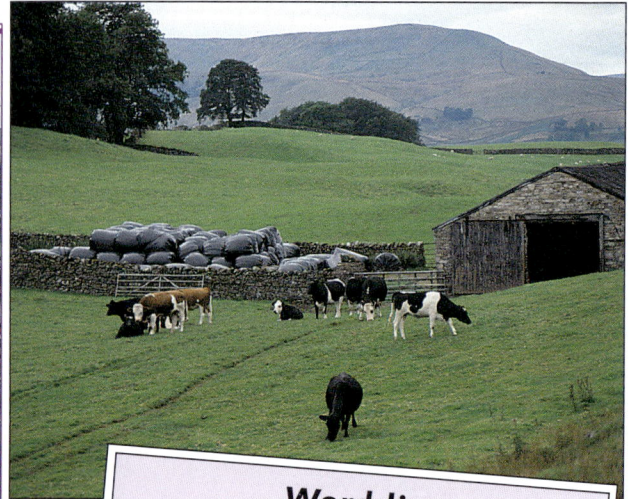

### Word list

| | |
|---|---|
| hill | wooden fence |
| river | canal |
| trees | beach |
| motorway | village |
| stone wall | sheep |
| bus station | factory |
| railway | lake |
| road | cows |
| city | sheep farm |

**Task**

1 Make a chart like this to show what you can see. Use the word list to help you.

| I can see | I cannot see |
|---|---|
| hill | motorway |
| | |

Now add some of your own.

**Key:**

- **n** National Park Centre
- ⋯ National Park Boundary
- **P** Car Park
- ⛺ Picnic Site
- ▲ Camp Site
- 🚐 Caravan Site
- ∪ Horse Riding
- ⛵ Sailing

Moudy Mea

more Forest · River Greta · ▲ Huggill Force · BOWES · Gilmonby · A66(T)

ite Stone Gill · Sleightholme Beck · Cleasby Hill 510 · Hoove 554 · Stang Forest

ightholme Moor

kengarthdale Moor 668 · Rogan's Seat 671 · ARKENGARTHDALE · Booze Moor 522

Friarfold Moor 589 · Great Pinseat 583 · Whaw · Langthwaite

Melbecks Moor · Reeth Low Moor 487

716 · Thwaite Common · Thwaite Beck · Angram 499 · Kisdon Hill · Thwaite · Muker · Ivelet · Gunnerside · Kearton · Healaugh

Buttertubs Pass · Muker Common · River Swale · Blea Barf 540 · Feetham · Low Row · SWALEDALE · Harkerside

Lovely Seat 675 · Crackpot · Whitaside Moor · Gibbon Hill

Abbotside Common 535 · Oxnop Gill · The Fleak 544 · 565 · Pickerstone Ridge · Apedale Beck

Askrigg Common · Woodhall Greets

High Shaw · Whitfield Gill Force · Newbiggin · Beldon Beck

Hardraw Force · Sedbusk ∪ · ppersett · HAWES · River Ure · A684 · Bainbridge · Askrigg · Woodhall

55 · ▲ P n · Gayle · Burtersett · Addlebrough 476 · Thornton Rust · Carperby · WENSLEYDALE

Drumaldrace 614 · Countersett · Semer Water · ⛺ Aysgarth · Aysgarth Force

Side · Bardale Beck · Stalling Busk · Stake Allotments · P n ⊕ ▲ · Thoralby · West Burton

Raydale Beck · Cragdale Moor 634 · Newbiggin · Harland Hill 536

Beck · ROTHDALE CHASE · Bishopdale Beck · B6160 · Walden · Ca

Horse Head 605 · Yockenthwaite · Waterfall · Kidstones · Buckden Pike 702 · Walden Head

LANGSTROTHDALE · Cray Waterfall

Horsehead Moor · Kirk Gill Moor 610 · Hubberholme

---

Look at these maps.

**2** Write down the names of three small settlements.

**3** Write down the name of a large settlement.

**4** Where do you think the people of Askrigg go shopping?

**5** A dale is a valley. Which dale is Askrigg in?

**6** Which river flows past Askrigg?

**7** Why do you think the road runs alongside the river?

**8** How many schools are there in Askrigg?

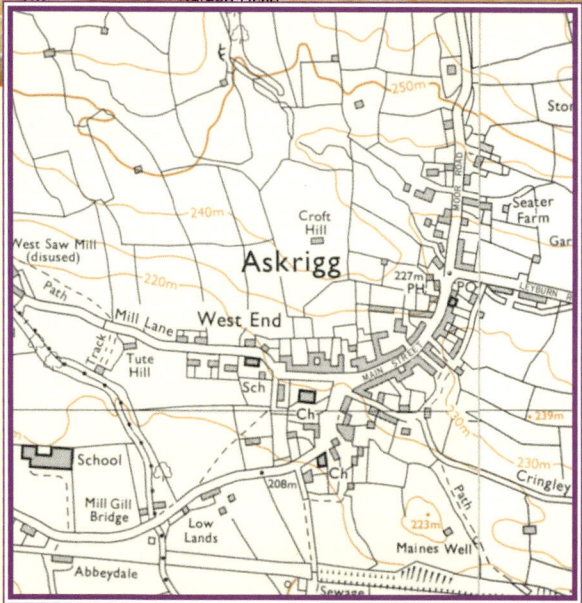

**9** Start in the car park north of the church. Turn left. What is the name of this lane? How do you think it got its name?

(Map of Askrigg)

250m · Stor · Br · West Saw Mill (disused) · 240m · Croft Hill · Seater Farm · Gar · 227m PH · **Askrigg** · 220m · Path · Mill Lane · West End · Track · Tute Hill · Sch · Ch · 239m · School · Ch · Cringley · Mill Gill Bridge · 208m · Low Lands · 230m · 223m · Maines Well · Abbeydale · Sewage

11

# 'Tomorrow will be hot and sunny'

## How hot is it going to be?

All these people are going on holiday for two weeks.

● Bob and Jan are going to Egypt.

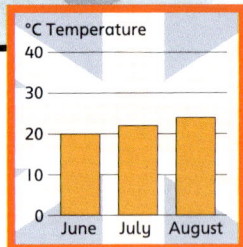

°C Temperature

● The Kelletts are staying in Britain for their holiday.

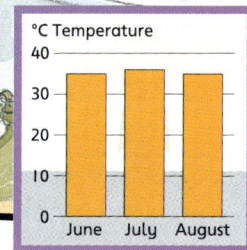

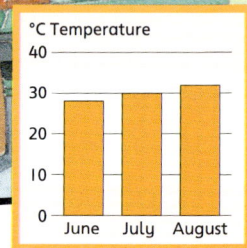

°C Temperature

These charts show what the hottest temperatures are likely to be.

● Laura and Mark are going to Spain.

°C Temperature

**Tasks**

1 I think _____ will have the most hot days because . . . . . . .

2 I think the hottest day will be in _____ because . . . . . . .

3 What do you think is in each suitcase? Copy the chart. Try to add some things of your own.

| Item | England | Spain | Egypt |
|---|---|---|---|
| T shirt | ✔ | ✔ | ✔ |
| Umbrella | | | |
| Sun hat | | | |
| Mosquito lotion | | | |
| Swimming costume | | | |
| Rain coat | | | |
| Sandals | | | |
| Sweater | | | |

Here are some photographs to show where the Kellett family, Laura and Mark, and Bob and Jan visited.

*Spain.*

*Britain.*

*The Sahara Desert.*

*Egypt.*

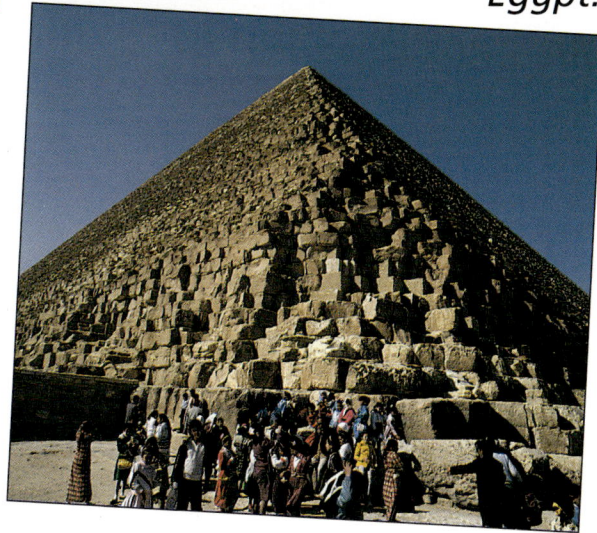

Tasks

4 Make a list of what you would do in each place.

Here are some ideas to help you:

**sunbathe    swim in the sea
go shopping    play ball games
look at interesting places**

5 Look at the photographs carefully, try to describe each scene. Think about
**buildings    clothes
plants and trees
colours**

6 The Sahara Desert is one of the hottest places in the world. Look at the photograph. Say why it would be difficult to have a holiday there.

*THINK about symbols*

A weather forecaster uses ☀ to show sunny weather in Britain.

Draw symbols of your own for Spain, Egypt and the Sahara Desert – think about how hot these places can be.

13

THE WEATHER

# 'Tomorrow will be cold'

## How cold is it going to be?

○ Aberdeen, U.K.

○ Antarctica

● The Alps, France

**Tasks**

1 Which place has the lowest temperature in January?

2 The coldest month in the U.K. is _____.
The coldest month in the Alps is _____.
The coldest month in the Antarctic is _____.

3 Describe what you can see in each photograph. Here are some things to think about
**colours  trees  buildings  clothes  people  activities  weather**

4 Write about the activities you do when it is cold. What games do you play? What clothes do you wear?

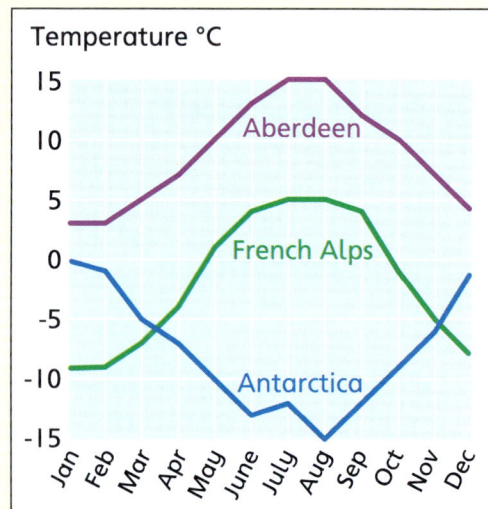

**THINK about symbols** A weather forecaster uses 2°C to show cold weather in Britain. Draw a symbol of your own for each of these places for a day in January.

Temperature °C — Aberdeen, French Alps, Antarctica

14

# 'Tomorrow will be wet'

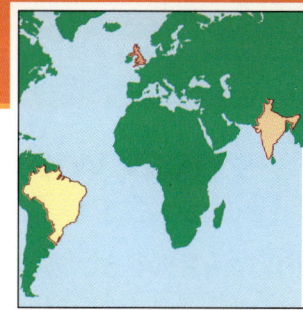

## How wet is it going to be?

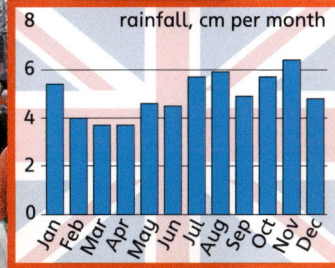

rainfall, cm per month

● In London, some days are wet and some days are dry.

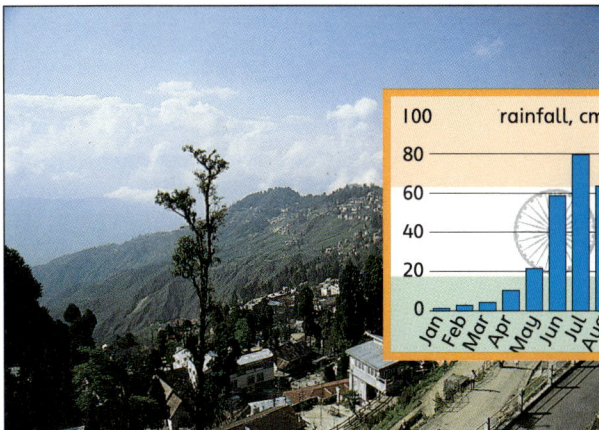

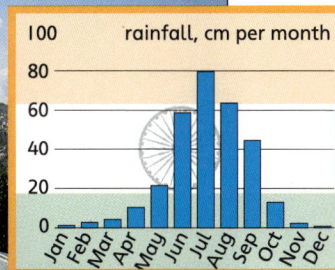

rainfall, cm per month

● This part of India can be very hot and dry. It also has a monsoon (rainy) season.

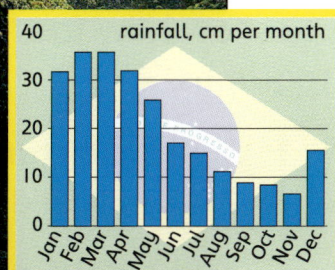

rainfall, cm per month

● In the tropical forests in Brazil it is hot and wet every day. There is only one season.

Tasks

5 Look at the photograph of London – what happens to the water?

6 Why do you think the houses are on stilts in this part of India?

7 Look at the the photograph of the tropical forest. Why do you think that the leaves stay green all the year round?

8 Look at the graphs. Which place has the most rain? (Look carefully at the *scale* of each bar graph.)

9 Which place has the biggest change in rainfall during the year?

10 Do deserts have high or low rainfall?

DRAW a symbol

A weather forecaster uses 🌧 to show rain. Draw symbols of your own for a wet day in each of the three places shown.

15

# 'Tomorrow will be windy'

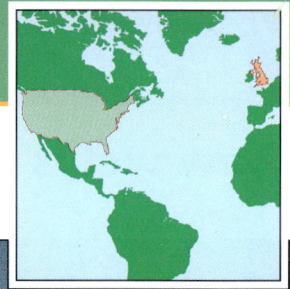

## How windy is it going to be?

In Britain we sometimes have strong winds which damage buildings.

In parts of America tornadoes can put people in danger.

Some people enjoy the wind.

Wind can be used to help us. These modern windmills are used to make electricity.

**Tasks**

1 The Beaufort Scale is used to show how fast the wind is blowing. Copy and complete this chart to show how fast you think the wind is blowing in each of the photographs.

| Force | Wind | Picture |
|---|---|---|
| 0 | calm | |
| 2 | light breeze | |
| 5 | fresh breeze | |
| 8 | gale | |
| 10 | storm | |
| 12 | hurricane | |

2 Draw pictures which show the wind speeds in the table.

3 Pictures C and D show two ways the wind can help us. Write or draw other ways the wind is used.

# A weather forecast includes temperature, rainfall and wind.

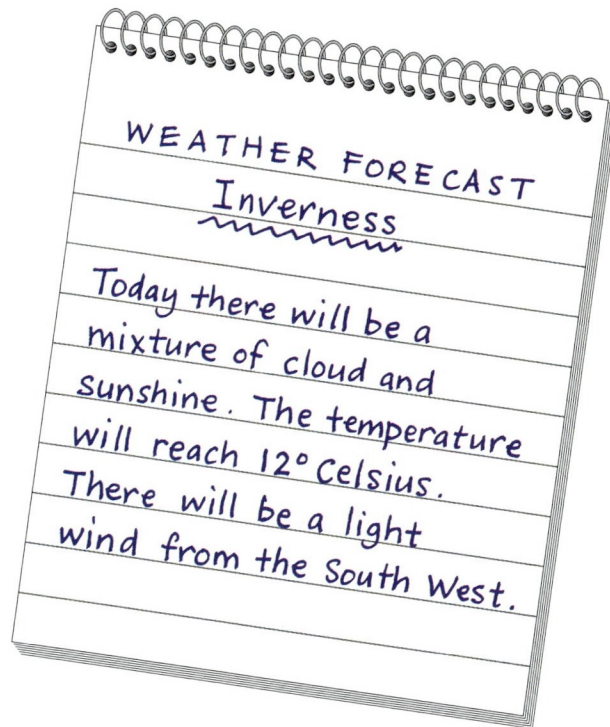

**WEATHER FORECAST**

**Inverness**

Today there will be a mixture of cloud and sunshine. The temperature will reach 12° Celsius. There will be a light wind from the South West.

4 Write a weather forecast for Manchester and Torquay. Put in as much information as you can.

5 Copy this chart and record what the weather is like today at your school.

| Date | |
|---|---|
| How hot or cold is it? (temperature) | |
| How wet is it? (rainfall) | |
| How windy is it? (wind speed) | |

Is there something else about the weather you can record?

6 Make a weather map to forecast what the weather will be like at your school tomorrow. Use your own weather symbols.

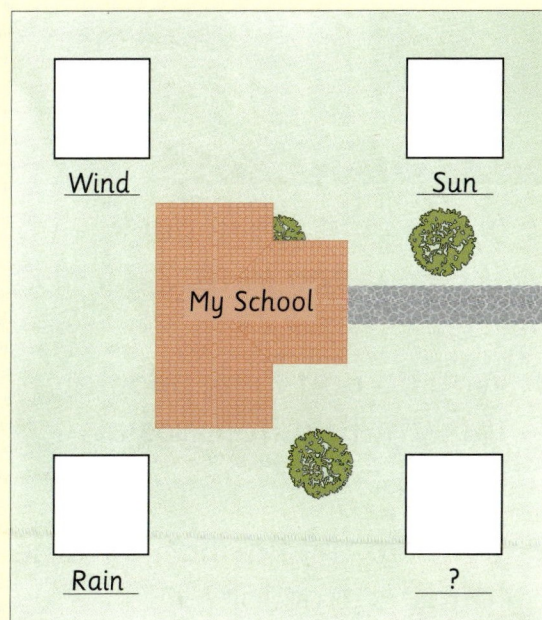

Wind

Sun

My School

Rain

?

# The growth of Brighton

## Why did Brighton grow as an important holiday town?

Brighton was Britain's first seaside holiday town. In 1750, Dr Richard Russell wrote a book about Brighton. He said that the sea air and swimming were good for you.

His book was read by George, Prince of Wales. George went to Brighton for his holidays and it became famous.

The prince built the Royal Pavilion as his summer palace. It was completed in 1822.

**Tasks**

1 Why do you think people thought Brighton was a healthy place?

2 Why did the Pavilion become a tourist attraction?

3 Which country does the Pavilion remind you of? Why?

4 Why do you think the Prince liked this design?

Posters were designed to encourage visitors to Brighton.

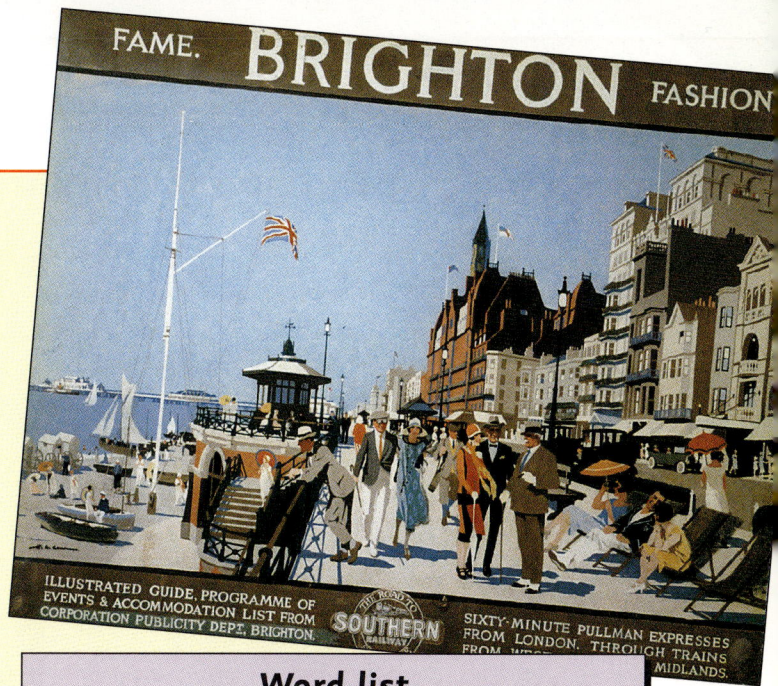

FAME. BRIGHTON FASHION

ILLUSTRATED GUIDE, PROGRAMME OF EVENTS & ACCOMMODATION LIST FROM CORPORATION PUBLICITY DEPT, BRIGHTON.

SOUTHERN RAILWAY

SIXTY-MINUTE PULLMAN EXPRESSES FROM LONDON. THROUGH TRAINS FROM WEST MIDLANDS.

**Tasks**

5  List the activities shown on the Brighton poster.

6  Which are still popular and which have changed?

7  Posters are designed to attract certain types of people. Look carefully at the poster. Sort these words into two lists:

a)  types of people to attract,

b)  types of people not to attract.

**Word list**

families   rich   fashionable   children
adults   poor   trendy   smart   famous
boring   dull   disabled   elderly   dowdy

These photographs show holiday attractions in Brighton in the 19th century.

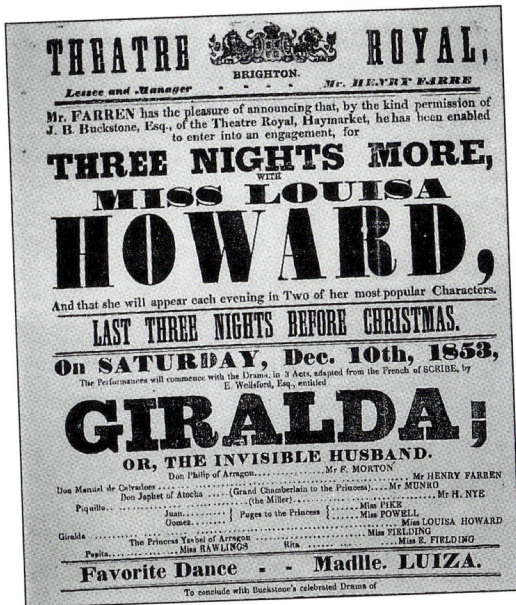

Theatre Royal, built in 1807 and still open.

The West Pier, built in 1866, now closed down.

**Tasks**

8  Why do you think a theatre was built?

9  Why might a theatre be attractive to tourists?

10  Why was the pier built?

11  Interview an adult you know well about a visit to a pier in the past.

BRIGHTON
A Coastal Town

## Has Brighton changed?

Brighton is still a holiday town. Some parts have changed and some have stayed the same. The Palace Pier is still open.

*The Palace Pier, built in 1899.*

The oldest part of Brighton is called **The Lanes**. This area has many cafes and shops.

### Tasks

1 Is this a modern photograph? How do you know?

2 How old is the pier?

3 What can people do on the pier?

4 Compare this scene with the poster on page 19. List the similarities and differences.

5 Will the pier manager prefer dry or rainy weather? Say why.

### Tasks

6 Why does Brighton have many cafés?

7 Compare The Lanes with a shopping area in your nearest large town.

Copy and complete the chart.

|  | The Lanes | Your shopping area |
| --- | --- | --- |
| road material |  |  |
| traffic |  |  |
| shop design |  |  |
| lighting |  |  |

8 Write what you like about The Lanes and what you dislike.

*The Lanes.*

Brighton Marina Village

The new marina is the biggest in Europe. It can hold 2000 boats. It has a sports centre and a fishing club.

*The beach is still important to visitors today.*

Tasks

9 Copy and complete the table which lists some of Brighton's attractions.

| Tourist attraction | 1900 | Today |
|---|---|---|
| Beach | | |
| Palace Pier | | |
| Theatre Royal | | |
| Marina | | |
| Seaside and sunshine | | |
| West Pier | | |
| Safe swimming | | |

# Brighton here we come!

## People travel to Brighton from many places.

People travel from far and wide to holiday in Brighton.

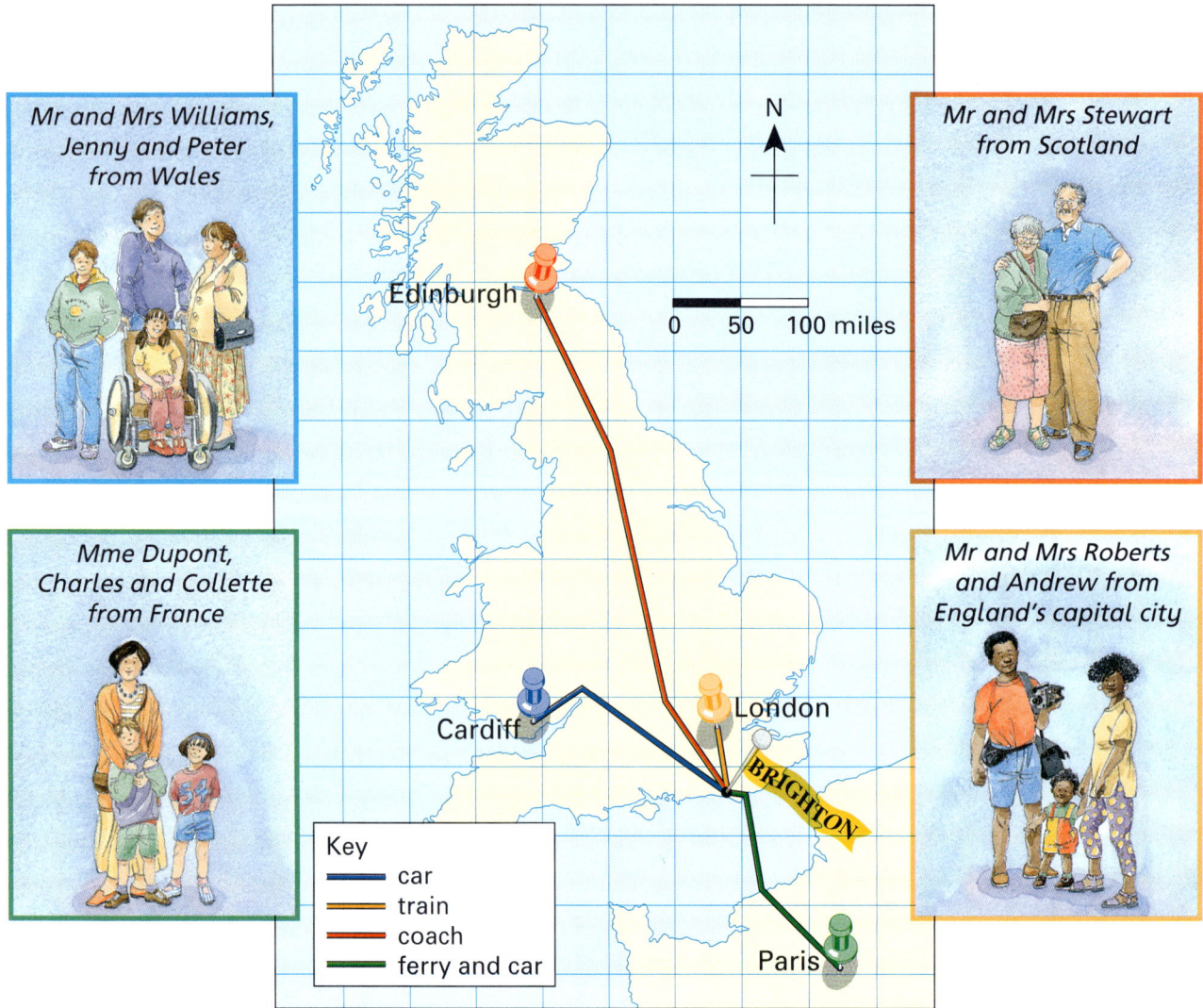

**BRIGHTON — A Coastal Town**

Mr and Mrs Williams, Jenny and Peter from Wales

Mr and Mrs Stewart from Scotland

N

0    50    100 miles

Edinburgh

Mme Dupont, Charles and Collette from France

Mr and Mrs Roberts and Andrew from England's capital city

Cardiff

London

BRIGHTON

**Key**

| | |
|---|---|
| —— | car |
| —— | train |
| —— | coach |
| —— | ferry and car |

Paris

**Tasks**

Copy and complete the journey chart.

1 Who had the fastest journey? Can you explain why?

2 Who had the slowest journey? Why?

3 How could the Dupont's journey take less time?

| Family | Home town | How travelled | Distance | Time taken |
|---|---|---|---|---|
| Williams | | | | 4 hrs |
| Roberts | | | | $1\frac{1}{2}$ hrs |
| Dupont | | | | 11 hrs |
| Stewart | | | | 9 hrs |

Brighton

**4** List the names of places which are linked to the Royal Family.

**5** Write the grid square for each place.

**6** In which grid square is the
a) Town Hall
b) Swimming pool
c) Theatre
d) Bus Station?

**7** Which tourist attractions are found in
a) E5
b) D3
c) A4
d) C3

# Beside the sea

## What do people do on the beach?

Look at the photograph of Brighton beach.

1 List four things you can see people doing.

2 Write three words which describe the weather.

3 Imagine you could spend a day on this beach. Write a diary for a day.

4 Think about danger. Make a chart like this:

| Danger | Reason |
|--------|--------|
| Water | non-swimmers could drown |
|  |  |
|  |  |
|  |  |

5 How will the beach change during the day?

This is a pictorial map of the beach.

Key:
- ☐ amusement arcade
- ☐ road for car parking
- ☐ beach for sunbathing
- ☐ safe water for swimming

Look at the map and photograph.

**6** Copy the key.

**7** Add the correct letter to each box in the key.

**8** Draw your own pictorial map of the beach.

**9** Make an activity key to show on your drawing:
  a) swimming
  b) sunbathing
  c) eating
  d) boating

# Living in Brighton

## Where do visitors stay?

Before going on holiday, each family sent for some information. The Tourist Office sent 'A Guide to Brighton'. These are four of the places to stay. The symbols give some information about each.

**2** SEA VIEWS - EN SUITE BATHROOMS
BED AND ENGLISH BREAKFAST FROM £20.00 pppn.
GRANVILLE HOTEL

|  |  |
|---|---|
| 🛁 | Bedrooms with private WC and bath |
| 📺 | Colour television in bedrooms |
| 🍼 | Baby minding facilities |
| 🛏 | Cots available |
| F | Family rooms available |
| C | Special rates for children |
| 🎠 | Children's facilities/playroom |
| ♿ | Suitable for disabled guests |
| P | Parking facilities |
| ♿A | Wheelchair access |

**1** 🍼 📺 🛀 🛏 F C 🎠 P

**Where to stay?**

**3** 🛁 📺 ♿ P ♿A

**4** Luxury self-catering apartments

## Tasks

Look at the details about each place.

*Mr and Mrs Roberts and Andrew*

1 Which would be the best for the Roberts family? Give two reasons.

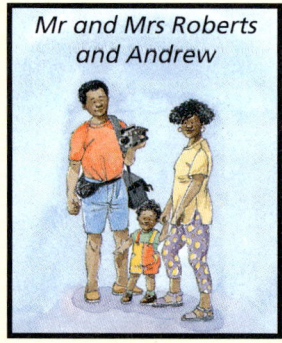

*Mr and Mrs Williams, Jenny and Peter*

2 Which would be the best for the Williams family? Give two reasons.

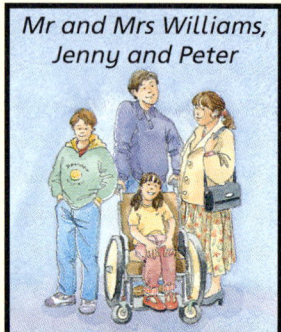

3 Where would you choose to stay? Say why.

26

Warmdean School is in Brighton. This is what some of the pupils say:

*I'm David. My mum is a teacher at my school. I like Brighton best in the winter when it is quiet.*

*I'm Susan. My parents own a small boarding house. They work very hard in the summer and autumn.*

*I'm James. My dad works on the pier but in the winter he has no job.*

*I'm Emily. My family has a gift shop in the Lanes. In the winter it is not very busy.*

*I'm Jason. My grandad never goes into town in summer. He hates the traffic and crowds.*

*I'm Jinchai. My mum works at the new conference centre which is open all year.*

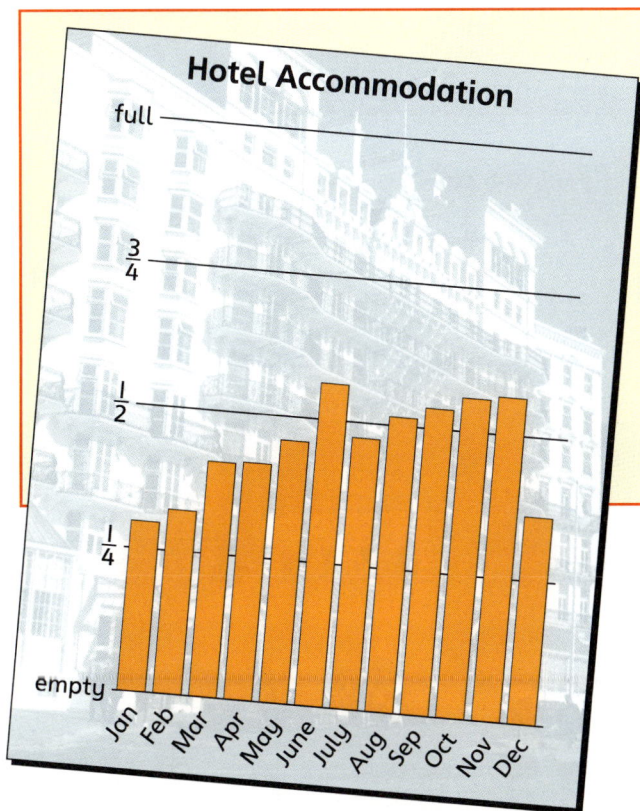

**Tasks**

**4** What problems does the holiday industry bring?

**5** How does the holiday industry help Brighton?

**6** Look at this chart. In which months are the hotels fullest? When are they less than half full?

### Hotel Accommodation

Bar chart showing hotel accommodation levels from empty to full. Y-axis marked: empty, $\frac{1}{4}$, $\frac{1}{2}$, $\frac{3}{4}$, full. X-axis: Jan, Feb, Mar, Apr, May, June, July, Aug, Sep, Oct, Nov, Dec.

Brighton's hotels used to be over half empty for longer. Now Brighton is an important conference town as well as a holiday town. It has over 1500 conferences a year.

LIVERPOOL
A Large City

### Large cities offer choice.

Michael O'Brien is eight years old. He lives in Liverpool. On Saturdays he likes to visit the city centre with his family.

Here are six photographs of places he has visited.

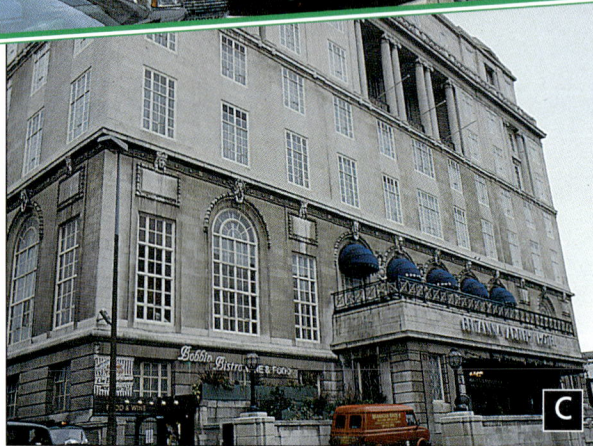

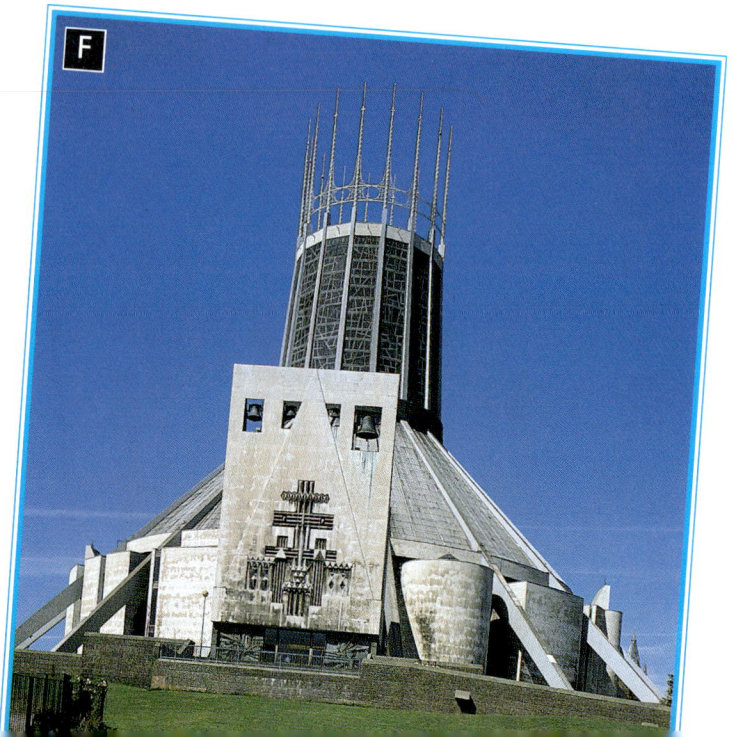

| Place | Letter | Main use | Jobs done |
|---|---|---|---|
| Anfield Football Ground | | | |
| Liver Building | | | |
| Albert Dock | | | |
| City shopping centre | | | |
| Adelphi Hotel | | | |
| Catholic Cathedral | | | |

Copy the chart.

1  Match the names of the places to the letters on the photos.

2  Choose from the list the main use of each place.

| shopping | worship |
|---|---|
| football | office work |
| tourism | eating and sleeping |

3  List three jobs done by adults in each place.

Look at the map below.

4  Write the grid reference for each place (except Anfield Football Ground).

5  List the grid squares you would pass through to each place. Always start at Lime Street railway station.

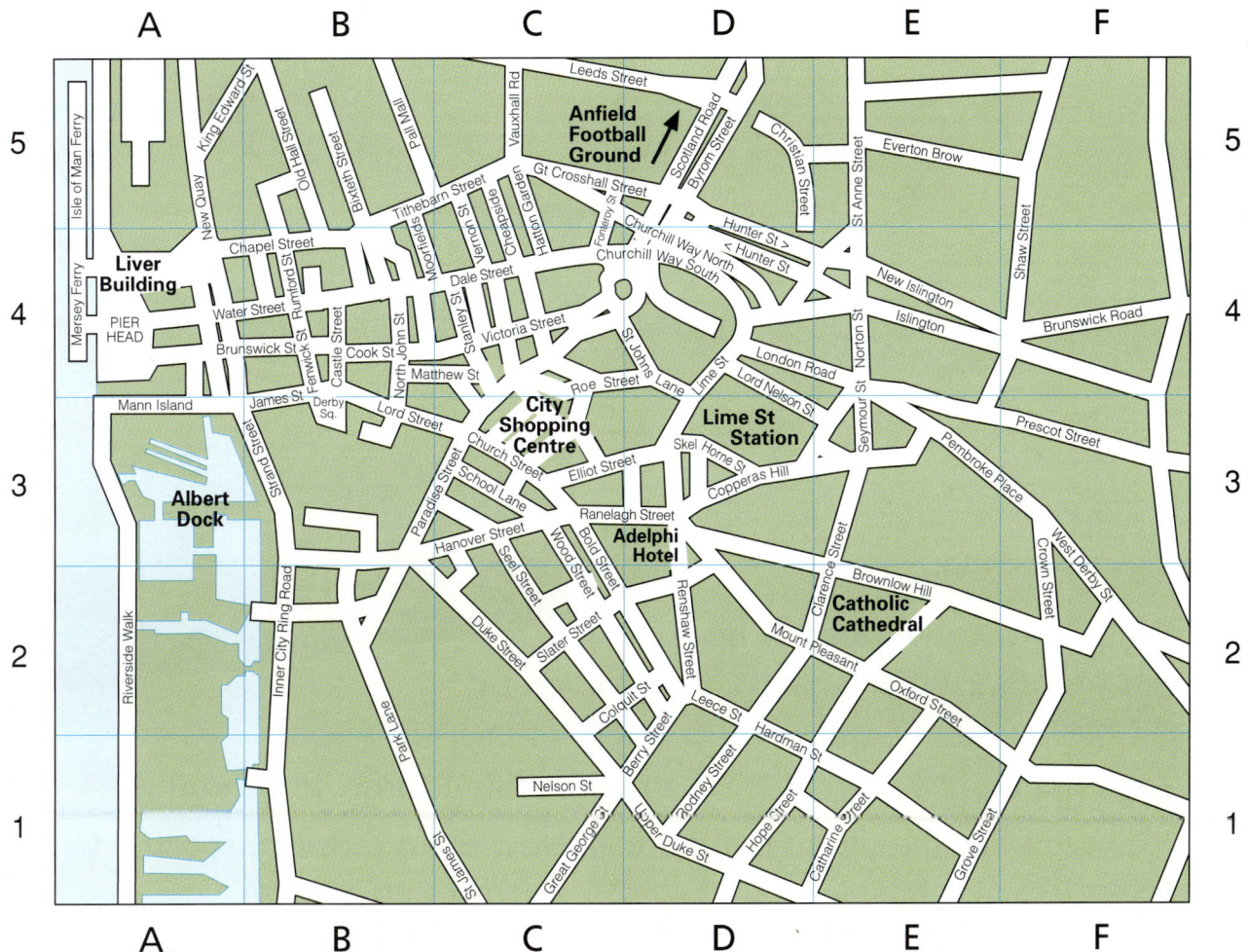

# What happened here?

The Shambles, York. At one time animals were killed in the Shambles, and their meat sold for food. Look up the word "shambles" in the Glossary. How is the name of this place connected with the present day's meaning of the word?

Cheapside, London. Any word like "cheap", "chap" or "chipping" meant that a town had a market. What other places do you know with this word in their name?

What connection can you find between "cheap" and "market"?

## Things to Do

**A** Make a list of the street names in your area. Put them in the order you think it was most likely they were built or named. For example, Church Street will probably be older than Railway Lane, because the Church was almost certainly built before the railway.

**B** Are there any streets near you named after trees, such as Lilac Avenue or Elm Lane? If so, find out if there ever were trees of that kind in the area.

**C** What do these names tell you about the towns?
*Oxford      Cambridge      Portsmouth      Crowland*
Make a list of towns near you with names that tell you about where they started or how they grew up.

**D** Get a street map of your nearest town. Using the information in this unit, mark in different coloured pencils the oldest parts. Then try to "date" the other parts. The clues below will help you.

TUDOR TIMES **(15th to 16th centuries)** low thatched cottages, larger town houses.

THE MIDDLE AGES **(11th to 15th centuries)** Castles, markets, guildhalls, gates.

MODERN TIMES Housing estates and supermarkets.

VICTORIAN TIMES

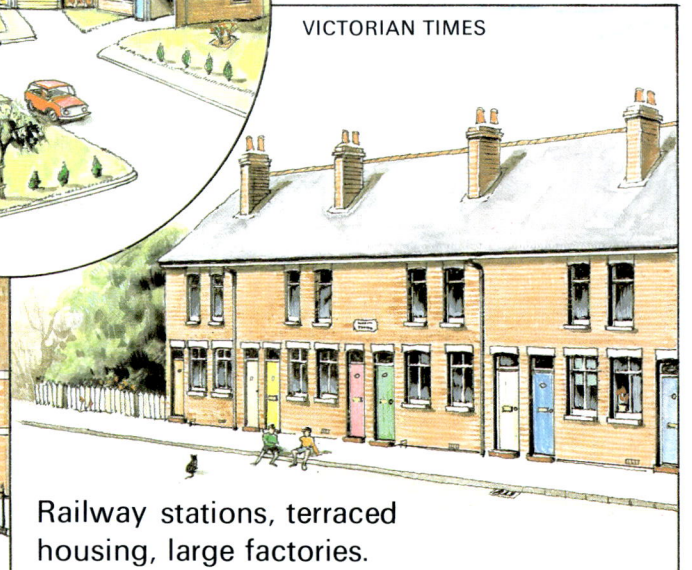

Railway stations, terraced housing, large factories.

GEORGIAN TIMES **(18th to 19th centuries)** Georgian houses, coaching inns, small factories, mines and mills.

# Who Are They?

## Statues

Statues are often put up in memory of people. They can give important clues about people of the past. Are there any statues near where you live? Who do they commemorate?

Queen Victoria's statue,
London

## Clocks

Sometimes famous people and events are remembered by clocks.

Statues and clocks are often called street furniture. Let us look at some other street furniture which can give us clues about the past.

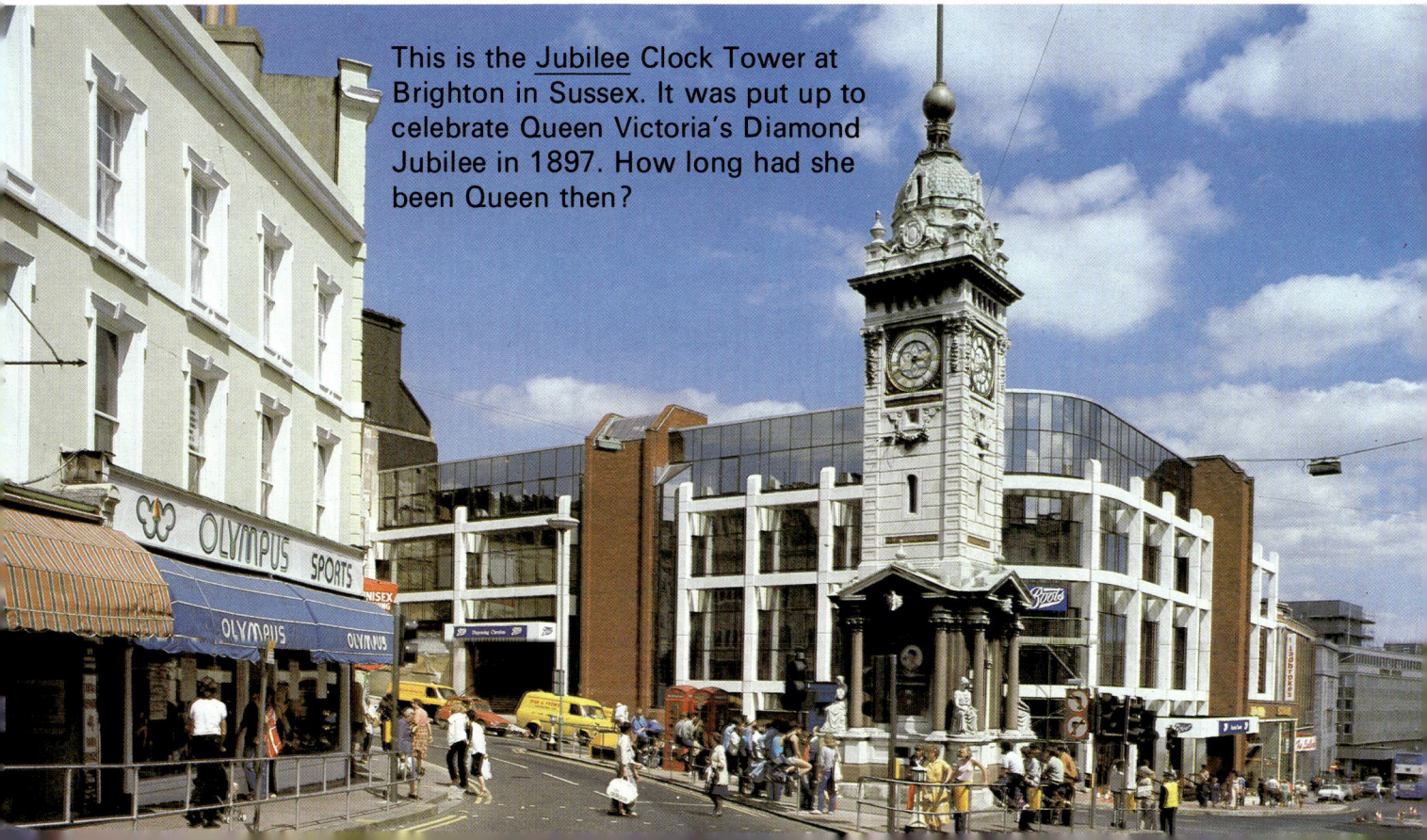

This is the Jubilee Clock Tower at Brighton in Sussex. It was put up to celebrate Queen Victoria's Diamond Jubilee in 1897. How long had she been Queen then?

# Pillar Boxes

In Book 1 you read about Rowland Hill who started the Penny Post in 1840.

The first pillar box appeared in the 1850s. Before that people took their letters to a post office.

There have been very few changes in the design of pillar boxes. The best clue to their age is the royal <u>cipher</u> on the front. For example, "VR" on the front of a box stands for "Victoria Regina". The "R" stands for "Regina" if there is a Queen and "Rex" if there is a King. They are Latin words.

This pillar box can be seen today in Chiswick, London.

Who was on the British throne when each of these pillar boxes was made?

Look at the ciphers. Remember, one king, George V, never had his number on a pillar box.

Here are the British kings and queens who have reigned since pillar boxes were first started.

Victoria
1837–1901

Edward VII
1901–1910

George V
1910–1936

Edward VIII
1936

George VI
1936–1952

Elizabeth II
1952 –

# Greyfriars Bobby

Statues and clocks are not always in memory of people. This dog statue is near Greyfriars Churchyard, Edinburgh. The dog's name was Bobby. There is a story that he used to come to Edinburgh on market day with a shepherd.

When the shepherd died, Bobby was so upset that he stayed by his grave for fourteen years. A local inn-keeper fed him each day. When "Greyfriars Bobby" died he was buried near the shepherd.

## Horse Troughs

This horse trough is at Burstow in Surrey. It was placed there in memory of horses which were killed or died of disease in the South African (or Boer) War (1899–1902).

Why do you think there is no water in it today? Why would horses not be used by soldiers in a modern war?

IN MEMORY OF THE MUTE FIDELITY OF THE 400,000 HORSES
KILLED AND WOUNDED AT THE CALL OF THEIR MASTERS
DURING THE SOUTH AFRICAN WAR 1899-1902
IN A CAUSE OF WHICH THEY KNEW NOTHING
THIS FOUNTAIN IS ERECTED BY A REVERENT FELLOW CREATURE

**A** Here are some statues. Find out who the people are and what they did. You are given a clue beside each one.

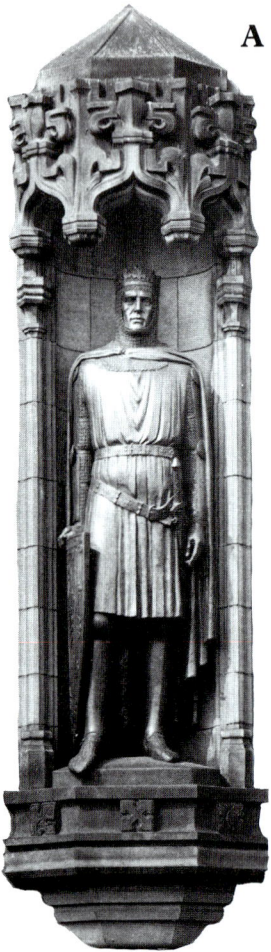

A lady who fought to get votes for women.

The first English seaman to sail round the world. He also fought against the Spanish Armada.

A famous Scots king who beat the English.

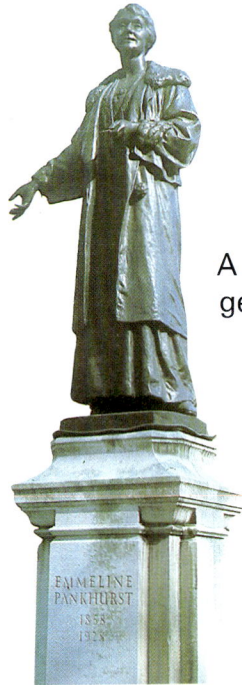

Britain's leader during the Second World War.

**B** One of the most famous clocks in the world has a bell called Big Ben. Where is the clock? How is it that people could hear Big Ben even when they are nowhere near it?

**C** Sometimes a house has a notice, or plaque, on the wall telling people that a famous person lived there. There are lots of plaques like this in London. Are there any near where you live? Who do they commemorate? Find out why these people are famous.

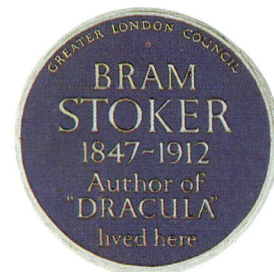

GREATER LONDON COUNCIL

BRAM STOKER 1847-1912 Author of "DRACULA" lived here

**D** Why do you think some letter boxes are called pillar boxes?

24  Answers to A. *The statues are of :* Robert the Bruce Emmeline Pankhurst Winston Churchill Francis Drake

# Signs of History

## Shop Signs

Long ago shopkeepers put up signs instead of having their name and the sort of shop written above the door. Why do you think they did this? The section below will give you a clue.

Can you tell what kind of shops these signs stood for?

## Inn Signs

Innkeepers gave their inns names which could be shown by a picture sign. In olden times most ordinary people could not read. They were told Bible stories and legends.

What old stories do these inn signs remind you of?

Who do Christians call "The Lamb of God"?

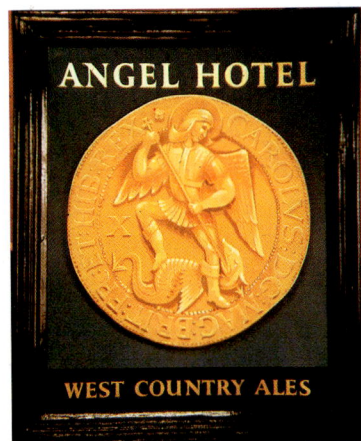

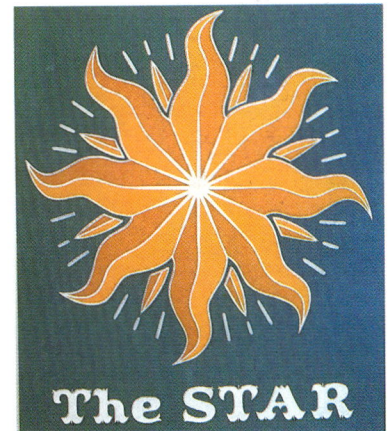

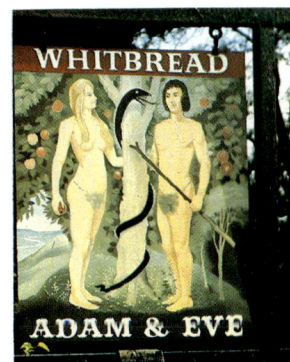

25

# Badges

Other inn signs may show the badge of a king or lord. Why do you think they had badges? This picture gives you a clue.

Is there an inn called "The Rising Sun" near your home? The Rising Sun was the badge of Edward III, who fought against the French at Crecy in 1346. Edward III was the father of the Black Prince whom you read about in Book 1.

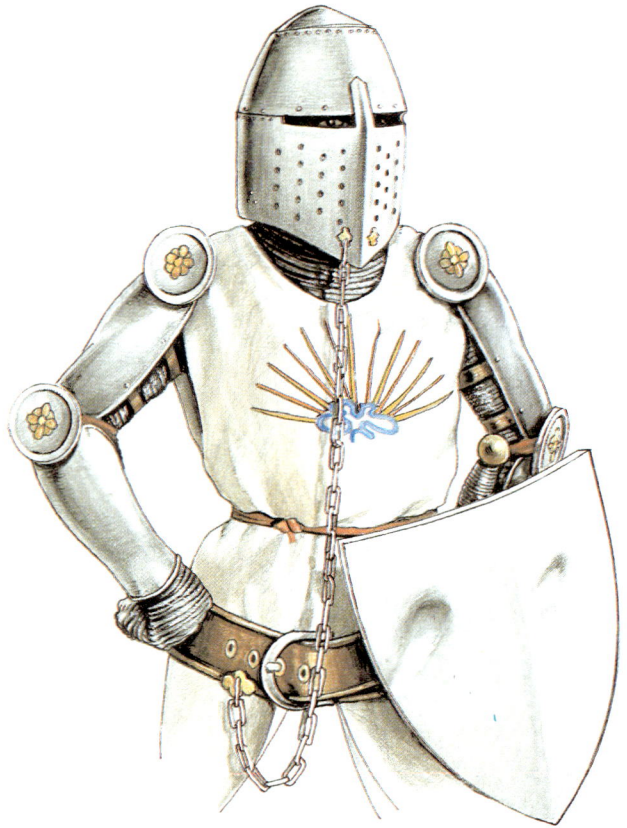

Here are some other kings with their badges. Do you know any inn signs with these badges?

Richard II

Henry V

Edward IV

## A Terrible Mistake

Even though soldiers had banners, or flags, with badges to show which side they were on, they sometimes made mistakes. The Battle of Barnet took place in 1471 during the Wars of the Roses. Edward IV's banner was a sun with a rose on it. His enemies had one showing a star with five long points.

It was a misty day and Edward's enemies mistook the star for the sun. So they shot off their arrows and killed some of their own men. So Edward won the battle.

## The Royal Standard

This flag also shows a royal badge. It is the <u>standard</u> of the Kings and Queens of Great Britain.

Some people say the animals in threes are leopards; some think they are lions. The first English king to use this animal on his badge was Richard the Lionheart (1189–99).

Where else might you see this flag flying?

NISI DOMINUS FRUSTRA

**A** Towns are given a badge or coat of arms when the king or queen gives the town a charter. The charter allows the town's people to run their own affairs. What do the shields on these badges tell you about Oxford, Aldeburgh and Edinburgh?

**B** Find out about the badge of your school or town. Where is it and what does it tell you?

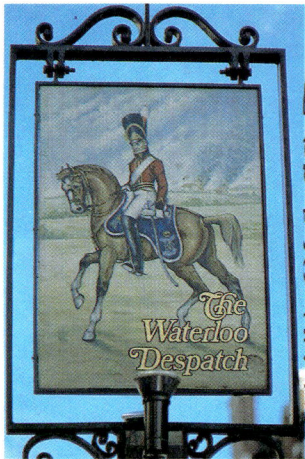

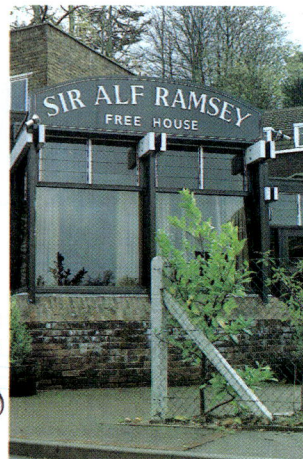

The Waterloo Despatch

WHITBREAD — CHURCHILL

SIR ALF RAMSEY FREE HOUSE

COACH and HORSES

**C** Above are some inn names. Find out about who or what they commemorate.

**D** Why did inns like this have a high arch and a yard at the back? Sometimes the clue is in the name – like this inn.

# Sport Around You

The Artful Dodger

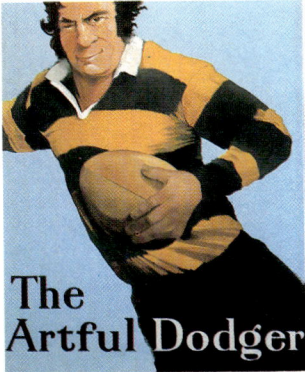

## Sporting Signs

Inn signs often refer to sports or pastimes. Look at these signs and see if you know the sport.

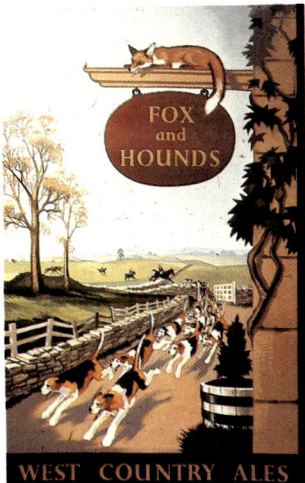

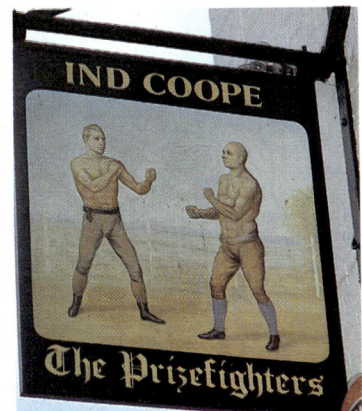

The Hand and Racquet

WATNEYS

SEA TROUT
FREE HOUSE

ACCOMMODATION
LUNCHEONS·DINNERS SERVED TO NON-RESIDENTS

FOX and HOUNDS

WEST COUNTRY ALES

IND COOPE

The Prizefighters

## Cricket

This sign is at the Bat and Ball Inn at Hambledon in Hampshire. Two hundred years ago Hambledon had one of the first cricket teams in England. The team met here and played matches on greens called Broad Halfpenny and Windmill Downs.

One Hambledon player, John Nyren, wrote a book called "The Cricketers of my Time". Find out about some of these old cricketers and how different cricket was then from the game played today.

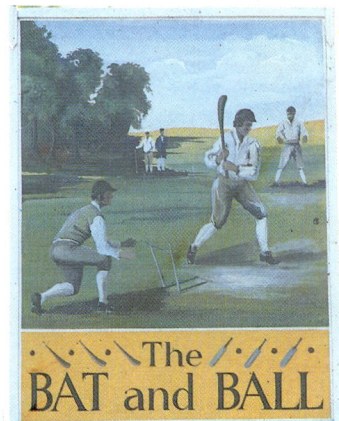

The BAT and BALL

# Football

## Football

Have you ever seen this kind of football played? Football is a very old game which was played by nearly all the men in the village. There were no rules and people were often hurt.

Rules were made for football about a hundred years ago. It was decided to play with eleven men on each side.

Many football teams have nicknames which give us clues about their past. For example, Arsenal are called "The Gunners". They have a gun on their badge because the team started in Woolwich Arsenal, and an arsenal is a factory for making guns.

How do you think these teams got their nicknames?

West Ham
– The Hammers.

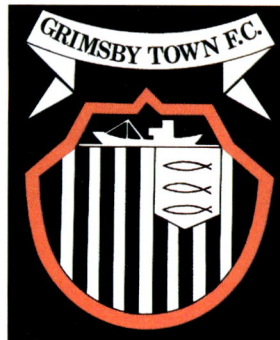

Grimsby Town
– The Mariners.

Now try explaining these:

| Football Team | Nickname |
| --- | --- |
| Stoke City | The Potters |
| Northampton Town | The Cobblers |
| Sheffield United | The Blades |
| Wolverhampton Wanderers | Wolves |
| Derby County | The Rams |

Do you remember why Everton football team is called "The Toffees" (Book 1)? Has your favourite football team got a nickname? What is it?

## What's the Game?

Over a hundred years ago a boy named William Ellis was playing football at Rugby school. He saw some bigger boys rushing at him. So, instead of kicking the ball he picked it up and ran away!

Here you see the game being played today. What is the name of the game?

## Things to Do

**A** Find out when the Football Association was formed. Where was the first Cup Final played? Who won?

**B** What happened when the Cup Final was first played at Wembley Stadium? The Oxford inn sign below gives you a clue about what happened *before* the game. Imagine you were at this game. What would you tell your parents about it when you came home?

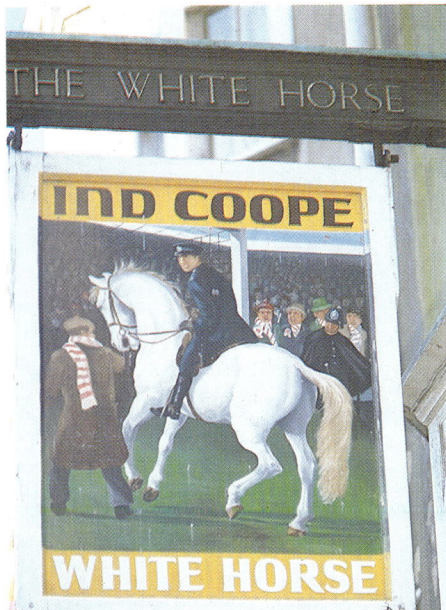

**C** Below are the badges of two universities. Each year they take part in the Boat Race. Find out when the Boat Race began. Who won the last Boat Race?

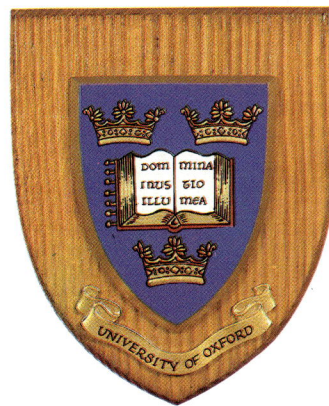

**D** Are there any inns or sportsgrounds near your town named after famous sportsmen or women? If so, who are they? Find out about these sportsmen and women, when they lived and what they did.

*W. G. Grace    Gordon Richards    Mary Rand*
*Mary Peters    Joe Louis*

# Schooldays Then and Now

The photograph below on the left shows the new Silverdale Church of England School in Staffordshire. The one on the right shows the old school which closed in 1980. It was built with money given by members of the Church of England, and was one of the first day schools for poor children in the area. The Church wanted them to be able to read the Bible and to write.

Most of these old schools were built in Victorian times (1837–1901). Until about a hundred years ago children did not have to go to school.

What differences can you see between the two schools?

Why do you think the old school has a bell tower?

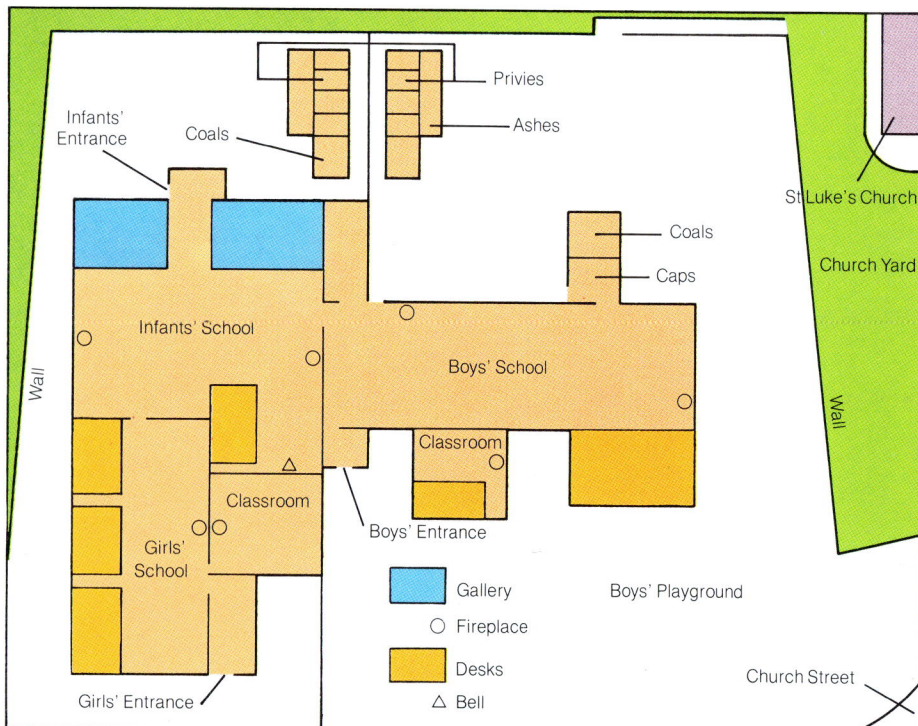

## Inside the School

The inside of the old school has been changed over the years. Here is a plan of what it looked like when it was built. Plans tell us a lot about schools in the past.

Look carefully at the plan. What do you think privies are? How was the old school heated?

Draw a plan of your school. How is it different from the old Silverdale School?

# In the Classroom

This picture shows children being taught in a gallery. Look at the plan on the right to see what a gallery was. Why do you think galleries were fitted in the classrooms? Can you think of a reason why classrooms do not have them today?

Look at the desks the children are sitting at. How are their desks different from yours?

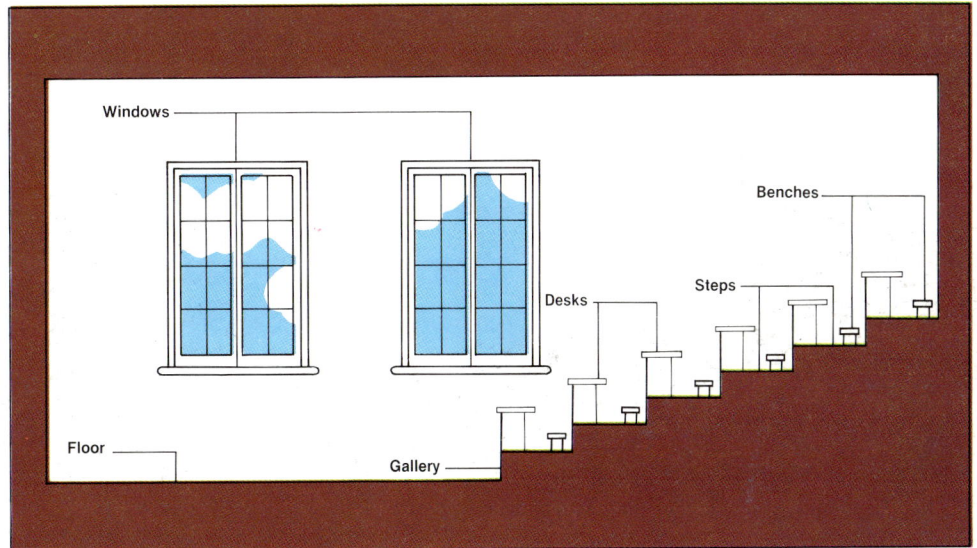

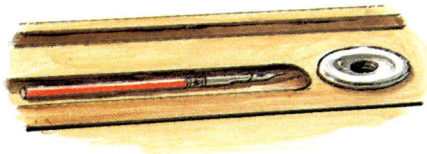

Here are some other objects used in old schools. Why are they rarely used today?

# Lessons in Victorian Times

Far fewer subjects were taught in Victorian times. This certificate
was given to a boy who left school over a hundred years ago.

*Sheffield Central National Scheme*

*The undersigned certify that*

*Charles Smith   aged 13   at the date hereof,
has attended the above named school for 7½ years
and that he can now read fluently, write a good hand,
work sums as far as Vulgar Fractions
and that his knowledge of*

| | | | |
|---|---|---|---|
| *Holy Scripture is* | *fair* | *Grammar is* | *good* |
| *Church Catechism* | *fair* | *English history* | *fair* |
| *Geography* | *fair* | | |

*During the whole time that he has been in the
above named school his conduct has been very satisfactory
and quite earnest in all respects.*

*Signed* --------------------------------

What are: *Holy Scripture   Grammar   Church Catechism?*
  What does Charles Smith's "good hand" mean?
  Make a list of all the subjects you learn which Charles Smith
did not learn.
  Would you have liked to go to school in Victorian times? If
not, say why.
  Notice how old Charles Smith was when he left school.
What is the school leaving age today?

# A Victorian Textbook

Here are two pages from the sort of text book Charles Smith would have used at school. It is called a Royal Reader.

It did not have as many pictures as a modern textbook. What other differences do you notice?

And the brooks wasted, and the cattle died ;
And good Elijah with his earnest prayer
Besought the Lord, till the consenting cloud
Gave rain, and thankful earth her fruits restored.

6. And then they sang a hymn ; and, full of joy,
The baby, crowing from his nurse's arms,
Came in and joined them, creeping merrily
After his little sister ; till, her pain
Of disappointment all absorbed in love,
She thanked her mother for the pleasant time
And for her tender lessons.

7.                    So that night,
Amid her simple prayer, they heard her say
Words of sweet praise to Him whose mercy gives
The blessed rain :—" For now I know, O God,
What pleases thee is best."

MRS. SIGOURNEY.

### New Words in this Lesson.

| | | | |
|---|---|---|---|
| ab-sorbed′ | de-cayed′ | E-li′jah | out′-stretched· |
| car-a-van′ | dis-ap-point′-ment | Is′-ra-el | wil′-der-ness |

### Notes and Meanings.

Ab-sorbed′, swallowed up.
Ag-o-ny, violent pain of body or mind.
Car-a-van′, a company of travellers.

Des′-erts, waste lands.
Droop′-ing, fainting ; hanging down their heads.
Grove, a small wood ; a group of trees.

No rain in Is′-ra-el. 1 Kings xvii., xviii.
Sad moth′-er. Genesis xxi. 14-21.
Wil′-der-ness, a wild or desert place.

**Summary :**—A little girl cried because it rained on her holiday afternoon. Then her mother told her how valuable the rain was, especially in Eastern lands ; and of Hagar, whose son was about to die of thirst, when the angel showed her a well of water ; and of Elijah's prayer to God for rain. So the child was satisfied that God knew what was best.

**Exercises :**—1. Parse : *A little girl cried because it rained on her holiday afternoon.*
2. Make Nouns from the following Adjectives—long, able, fair, quiet, selfish, silent, swift, mean, firm.
3. Describe the uses of Rain.

### TRY AGAIN.—I.

1. "Oh! try again, father, try again!" What a sad, pleading voice uttered these words! what a pale, little face was turned towards Peter Parsons, as he sat resting his head on the table!

"It's no use trying to give it up; I have tried, and I can't do it," was the father's dogged, despairing reply. "I know drink will be my ruin, but though it were poison, I must have it!

2. "Mr. Barker, my employer, gave me warning yesterday. He said he couldn't stand my habits any

Why are the items on the left hand page given the title "The Rain Lesson"?

Today when we say "caravan" we usually mean a mobile home. What different meaning of "caravan" is mentioned on the left hand page of the Royal Reader?

Look at the picture on the right hand page. What things in it make you think the scene happened long ago?

What did the father say would be his ruin?

**A** Charles Smith did not have large fields to play in like most modern school children. He had to play in the playground. These are the sorts of games Charles and his young sister might have played:

*skipping    hoops    jacks (or fivestones)
whip and top    marbles    hopscotch*

Have you ever played them?
Which of these games are still common today?
How do you play them?

**B** Has your school an old log book? It was a book in which the head teacher wrote down the more important happenings in the school. It was a sort of diary.

Read the entry on the right from a school log book of 1888. What jobs do you think teachers did then that they do not have to do today?

**C** Make a model of a gallery like the one at Silverdale. Use match boxes to build up the staging.

**D** Find out what it was like in the past at Eton, Harrow or Rugby where many boys who had rich parents went to school.

*E. Abrahams (a teacher) had not lighted her fire, dusted the room nor arranged the forms, children crying with cold*

# Going Shopping

## Markets and Fairs

Does any town near you still have a market? Perhaps you know a town which does not have one now, but did have one in the past. What place names or street names might tell you this? (See Unit 4.)

Most towns had a market every week. Farmers used to sell their sheep and cattle at markets. They also bought pots, pans, tools and ploughs there.

Louth market, Lincolnshire today.

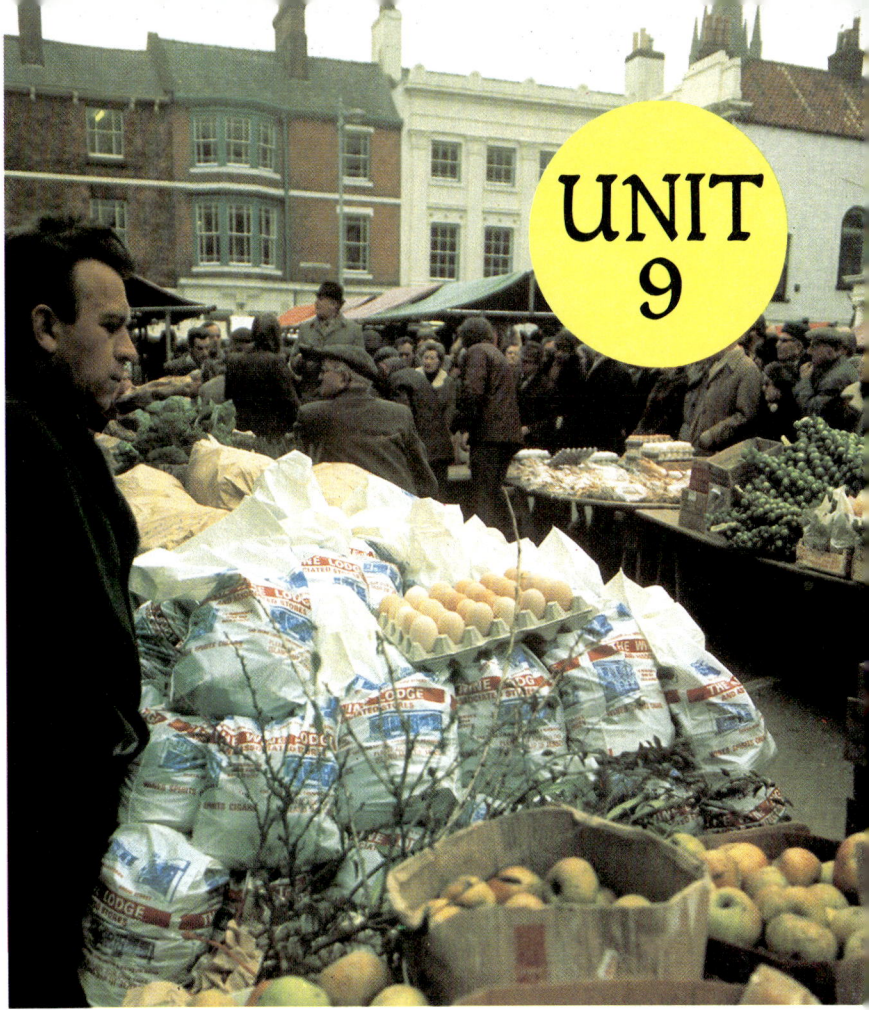

There were also giant markets, called Fairs, which were held in large towns once a year.

Fairs were times of fun too, with jugglers and other performers entertaining the crowds.

St Giles Fair, Oxford

# Making Goods to Sell

Years ago shopkeepers were also craftsmen. They made the goods they sold in their shops.

They made pots, pans and even ploughs for the farmers who came to town. They also made many other things, such as clothes, shoes and jewellery. We still call a place where things are made a *workshop*.

Today there are still a few shops where goods are made. What is this craftsman making? Have you a shop like this near where you live?

Factory making roller-skates

Department store in London

About two hundred years ago factories began to make lots of goods. There was no need for a shopkeeper to make what he would sell.

Of course, small shops never died out completely. But some businesses began to sell lots of different things. We call such shops "department stores".

Some shopkeepers became rich through running department stores. One who did was an American called Frank W. Woolworth. Everything in his stores was sold very cheaply.

In Britain, Woolworth stores at first sold nothing over 6d. What is 6d in modern money? You could buy a pencil for under 1d then. How much would one cost today?

## Twentieth-century Shopping

Today we shop quite differently from the way our grandparents and great grandparents did. Look at the pictures below. Compare the photograph of a store in about 1900 with the one of a modern supermarket.

These pictures will give you a clue to the two main differences between shopping then and shopping today.

**A** These photographs were taken in the Castle Museum at York. They show us how a street and shops looked about two hundred years ago. Have a good look at them and then answer the questions.

1. How would these streets be lit at night?
2. What would we call a druggist today?
3. One shop has the royal badge over the door. Why do you think this was?
4. What do we call this kind of street surface?
5. What was the square box with poles?
6. What was it used for?

**B** Imagine you are taken shopping in this street. Write about it for your diary.

**C** For centuries many goods were sold by street sellers. Each one had a special cry to tell people what was being sold. The picture on the right is still used today. The woman's cry was "Won't you buy my sweet lavender?" What sort of products have historical pictures on them today?

# Meeting Places

## Town Halls

Below is a <u>mayor</u> going in a procession
to the Town Hall.

Do you know why mayors dress in such old
fashioned clothes? It is because in the Middle Ages
most towns were run by merchants and this is the
way a merchant of that time dressed.

Can you see the chain round the mayor's neck? It
is called his "chain of office". It tells people that he is
the mayor of his town.

What is the man in front of the mayor carrying?

There have been town councils for a long time,
so there are some very old town halls.

Town Hall, Abingdon,
Berkshire. This hall
was built over three
hundred years ago.
What do you think
the space underneath
was used for?

Moot Hall, Aldeburgh,
Suffolk. This hall is even
older than Abingdon's.
It gets its name from
the Saxon word "moot"
meaning a meeting.

# Council Chambers

Go and visit your nearest town or city hall. That is where the town council holds its meetings. Quite often it will have drawings, photographs and other things telling of the past in your area.

In Scotland, District Councils have taken the place of Town and City Councils. The person who does the mayor's job there is usually called the provost.

A modern council has a lot of jobs to do. What clues to the jobs does this picture give you? Can you think of other jobs done by the council?

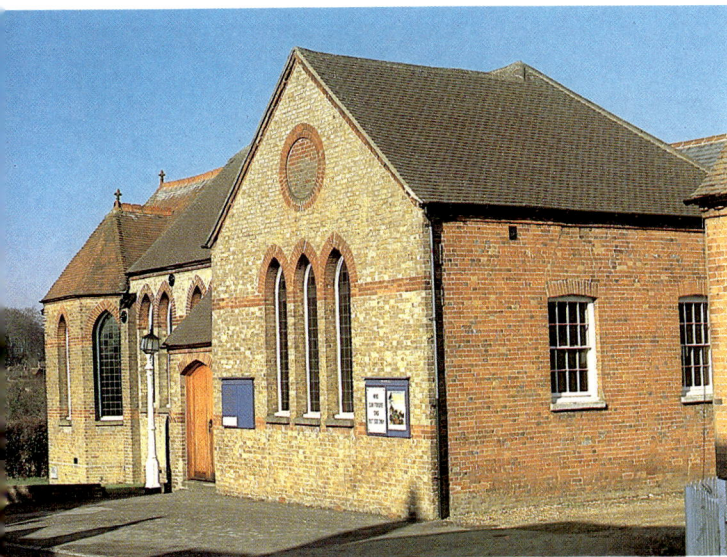

# Church Halls and Meeting Places

Your town may have other meeting places besides the town hall. Above is the Methodist Church Hall at Penn in Buckinghamshire. The Methodist Church was started as the result of the work of John Wesley, a preacher who lived over two hundred years ago.

John Wesley and his brother Charles formed a "Holy Club" when they were at University. Some students made fun of them because they kept to a strict time-table of prayers and Bible readings. The students called them "methodists".

This is the Friend's Meeting House at Jordans in Buckinghamshire. The Society of Friends are a Christian group who have a nickname. They are called "Quakers" because people said they quaked with fear when they thought of God!

Quakers are peaceful folk who refuse to fight in wars.

Some Quakers first met here in 1688.

Why do you think this fake wooden gun on *HMS Victory* is called a Quaker?

# Scout and Guide Huts

This is Robert Baden-Powell who started the Boy Scouts. He fought in the Boer War (1899–1902), and helped to defend a town called Mafeking against the enemy. Before that he had been an Army Scout, and rode ahead of the main army to check on the ground and spy on the enemy.

He did not want to make soldiers out of the boys. He thought they would enjoy the open air life which he had enjoyed when he was in the army. In 1907 he took a group of boys to camp on Brownsea Island in Poole Harbour, Dorset. A year later the Boy Scouts were started.

Scouts from many countries gathered together at Nordjamb, Norway in 1975.

In 1910 a similar organisation was formed for girls. What was it called?

Inside a Guide Hut.

Venture Scouts helping with younger members of the Scouts.

# A Famous Hall

You will remember reading about the Royal Festival Hall in Book 1. Here is a picture of an older hall in London. It is also used for concerts and other meetings of large numbers of people.

It was built in memory of Queen Victoria's husband and is named after him. What was he called? You could get some clues from the Street Directory on page 10 and the Things to Do on page 18.

---

## Things to Do

**A** Find out about the halls and meeting places in your area. How many local organisations (Women's Institutes or Townswomen's Guilds, Boy Scouts, Girl Guides and Church groups) meet in them?

**B** Is there a hall in your area named after a person? If so, find out about that person.

**C** The Festival of Britain was held in 1951. There were large displays of arts and crafts, both at a special site in London and all over the country. Did your town have a fair, a pageant or a play for this Festival?

Celebrations also took place for the Queen's Coronation in 1953 and her silver Jubilee in 1977.

Find out about these celebrations by asking older people, or visit the local library to look for photographs, programmes and other souvenirs.

**D** Some halls and libraries are named after Andrew Carnegie. He was the son of a poor Scots weaver who went to America where he made steel and became very rich. Find out more about him, and find out why some buildings in Britain are named after him.

Royal Festival Hall, London

# Poppy Day

## Remember the Dead

Have you ever noticed that the second Sunday in November is called Remembrance Sunday? November was chosen because the First World War ended in November, 1918. On that day men and women who served in the forces parade in front of their local war memorial. They do this to show that they are remembering those who were killed in two World Wars.

1914 – 1918
1939 – 1945

The Royal British Legion is made up of people who served in the forces. They hold a big meeting or rally in the Albert Hall on Poppy Day. Poppy Day is on the Saturday before Remembrance Day.

Poppies grow on the battlefields of France and Belgium where the British Army fought in two World Wars. So the poppy was chosen to remember those who died.

The picture on the left shows the two minutes' silence at the rally. During it over a million poppies float down from the roof. There is one poppy for every British person killed in the two wars.

Poppies are sold all over Britain each November. What do you think the money this brings in is used for?

This special monument, called the Cenotaph, stands in Whitehall, London. On Remembrance Sunday the Queen and Members of Parliament lay wreaths against the Cenotaph.

Buglers play a tune called The Last Post.

## The Unknown Warrior

The picture on the right shows the tomb of the unknown warrior in Westminster Abbey, London.

When the First World War ended, a British general was blindfolded and led into a hut. There were six coffins in the hut. Each one contained the body of a soldier who had been killed on a different part of the battle-front. The general touched one of the coffins. It was brought to England and buried in Westminster Abbey.

Nobody knows this soldier's name. He stands for all those killed in the wars.

BENEATH THIS STONE RESTS THE BODY
OF A BRITISH WARRIOR
UNKNOWN BY NAME OR RANK
BROUGHT FROM FRANCE TO LIE AMONG
THE MOST ILLUSTRIOUS OF THE LAND
AND BURIED HERE ON ARMISTICE DAY
11 NOV: 1920, IN THE PRESENCE OF
HIS MAJESTY KING GEORGE V
HIS MINISTERS OF STATE
THE CHIEFS OF HIS FORCES
AND A VAST CONCOURSE OF THE NATION

THUS ARE COMMEMORATED THE MANY
MULTITUDES WHO DURING THE GREAT
WAR OF 1914-1918 GAVE THE MOST THAT
MAN CAN GIVE LIFE ITSELF
FOR GOD
FOR KING AND COUNTRY
FOR LOVED ONES HOME AND EMPIRE
FOR THE SACRED CAUSE OF JUSTICE AND
THE FREEDOM OF THE WORLD

THEY BURIED HIM AMONG THE KINGS BECAUSE HE
HAD DONE GOOD TOWARD

The war memorial plaque, City of London School.

## Memorial Plaques

Most schools, colleges, offices, banks, post offices and railway stations have war memorials like this. They list the former pupils or workers who died in the two World Wars.

Are there any memorials like this near where you live?

## Two Minutes' Silence

At 11 am on 11th November, 1918 the First World War ended. For the first time for four years the guns were silent. People decided to remember this moment every year with a two minutes' silence. There was complete silence in most places of work, in schools and in the streets.

After World War Two it was decided to have the silence at eleven o'clock on Remembrance Sunday instead.

The two minutes' silence in 1926. Even the traffic stopped in London's Oxford Circus!

**A** Sometimes a chapel may be built as a memorial. This one is at Biggin Hill in Kent. It was built in memory of the airmen who flew from Biggin Hill during the Battle of Britain in 1940. They were fighting the German Air Force. The plane standing in front of the chapel is a Hurricane. Can you find out the name of any other planes used in the Second World War? Your parents or grandparents may be able to help you.

**B** Imagine you were a soldier when the First World War ended. Write down an entry in your diary about it.

**C** Describe or draw a war memorial near your home. Write down some of the names on it. Perhaps they are related to someone you know.

Are the people who died in both world wars listed on it? Were more people killed in the First World War or the Second World War?

War Memorial, Amersham, Bucks

**D** Write out and complete these sentences.
The tomb of the . . . . . . . . . . . . . . . . . . . . . . . . . . . . . . . . . . is in Westminster Abbey.
On Remembrance Sunday the Queen lays a wreath on the

. . . . . . . . . . . . . . . . .
The First World War ended on . . . . . . . . . . . . . . . . .

# Snakes and Crosses

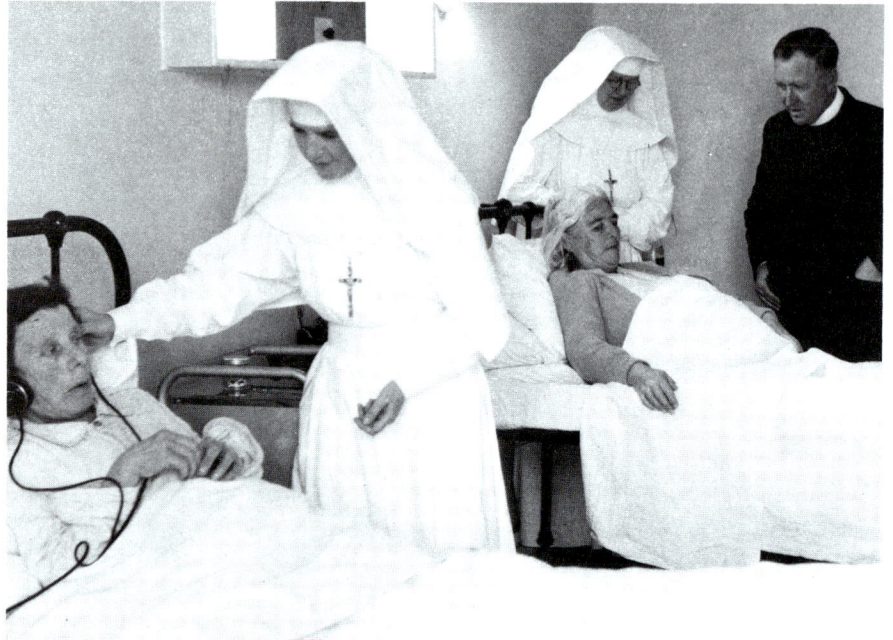

## Crosses

Have you ever thought why senior nurses are called "Sister"? Or why nurses wear white caps? This picture gives you a clue.

For hundreds of years most nursing in Christian countries was done by nuns. Nuns call each other "Sister" and wear white caps.

Nuns and monks were expected to heal and nurse the sick, as Jesus did.

## Snakes

The Greeks believed that Apollo and his son, Asklepios, were the gods of health. Temples were built to Asklepios. Harmless yellow snakes lived in one of these temples. The Greeks believed that these snakes brought good health. Ever since then a snake sign has been the badge of doctors and nurses. This explains why there is a snake sign on the round tower in the picture below

The Queen Victoria Hospital, East Grinstead, Sussex. (On the next page you can read about earlier hospitals in East Grinstead.)

# How One Hospital Grew

The picture above shows the first hospital in East Grinstead. It was opened in 1863 by John Rogers, a doctor.

Later, local people collected money and bought the larger house on the right.

Such hospitals for the poor were called "Cottage Hospitals". Why do you think this was?

# It Started with Peanuts

In 1931, money was being raised for a new hospital at Tunbridge Wells, Kent. A young lady newspaper reporter had an idea. She called herself "Aunt Agatha", and offered a bag of peanuts to any child who collected twelve pennies dated 1931.

Aunt Agatha's name was really Mrs. Gordon Clemetson. She had only been joking. But, to everybody's surprise, a little girl called Dorothy Jolley walked into a Tunbridge Wells bank with a bag of 1931 pennies.

So began the world famous Peanut Club, which later collected money for the children's ward at East Grinstead.

A child who has been treated for burns gets a "golden peanut".

The Peanut (Children's) Ward at Queen Victoria Hospital, East Grinstead.

# Guinea Pigs

During the Second World War many airmen were badly burned when their planes crashed. They were treated at Queen Victoria Hospital by a clever <u>surgeon</u> called Archibald McIndoe.

He used "plastic" surgery (using skin from other parts of the patient's body) to cover the scars left by the burns. It was a new method, so McIndoe called his patients "guinea pigs". Why do you think he called them this?

# Canadian Help

Some of the injured airmen came from Canada.

The part of the hospital shown here is called the Canadian Wing. It was built with money given by the Canadian Air Force. Why do you think the Canadians did this?

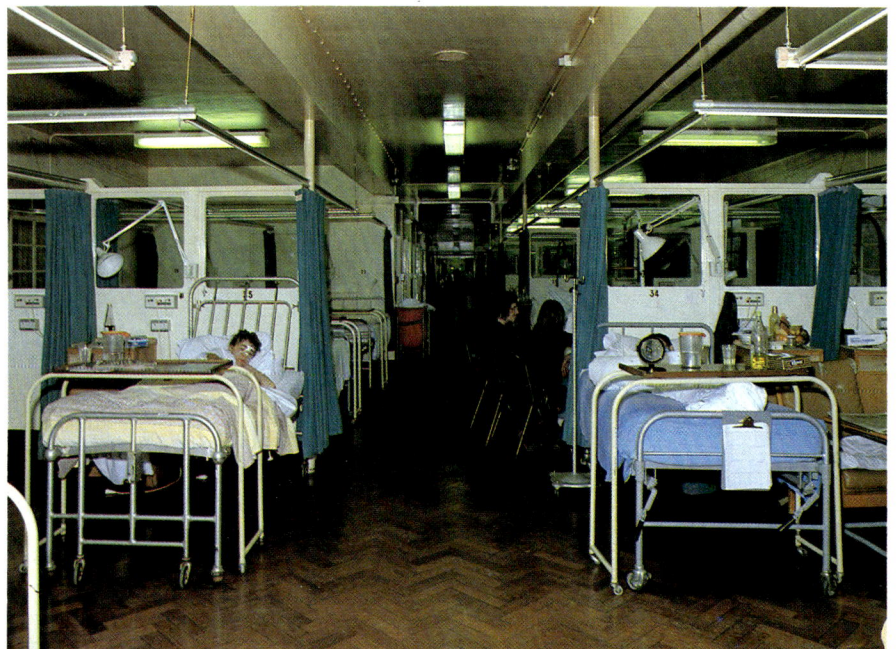

**A** Find out if there are any stories behind your local hospital. There may be wards and even beds named after people. Find out why.

**B** In 1859 a Swiss man called Henri Dunant saw the sufferings of wounded soldiers after a battle. He wrote about what he had seen. People who read the book decided to try and help. They held a meeting and formed the Red Cross organisation to help war victims. Find out what you can about the Red Cross in your town.

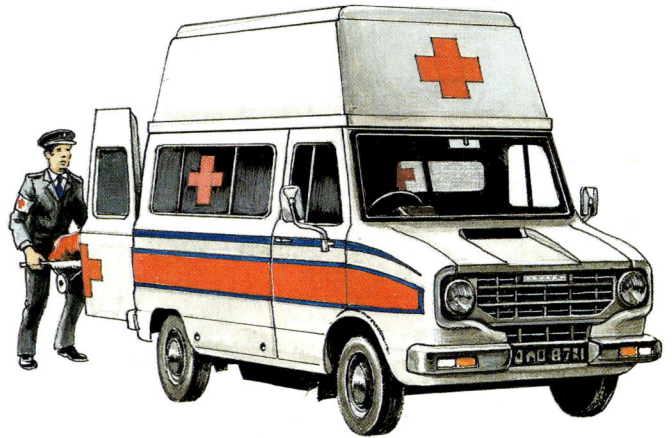

**C** How have operations changed in the last hundred years? These pictures will give you a clue.

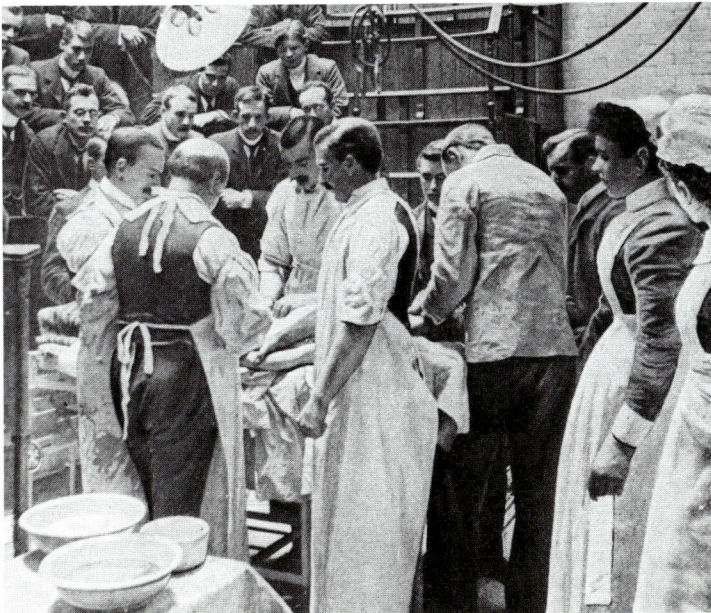

An operation in 1901

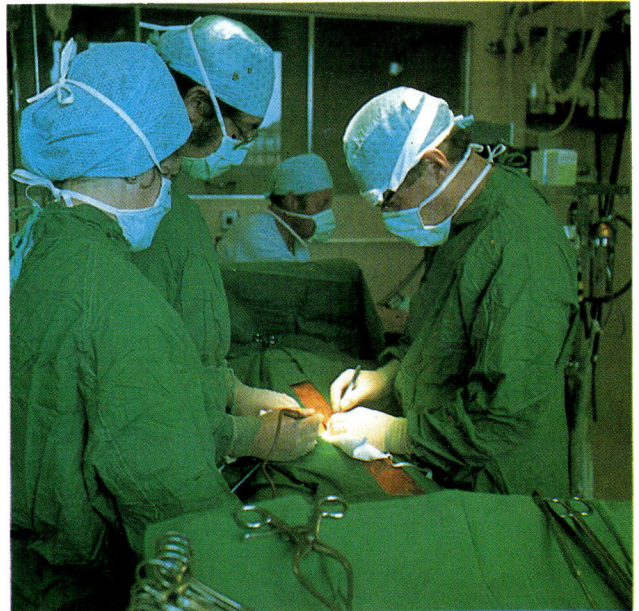

An operation today

**D** Many hospitals began as workhouses, or places where old or sick people and orphans had to live if they could not manage on their own. Find out more about workhouses and whether any of your local hospitals began as workhouses.

**E** You will remember reading about Alexander Fleming in Book 1. His discovery of penicillin was a very important step forward in curing certain infections. The work of Florence Nightingale and Joseph Lister was also important in the history of medical treatment. Try to find out more about them.

# Indoor Shows

These children are watching an old film on TV. Where do you think this old film was first shown? There is a clue in the picture below.

Many more people went to the cinema before TV was invented. There were special Saturday morning shows for children.

Here you see members of a "Saturday Club" paying to see westerns, adventure films and cartoons. This photograph was taken in 1948.

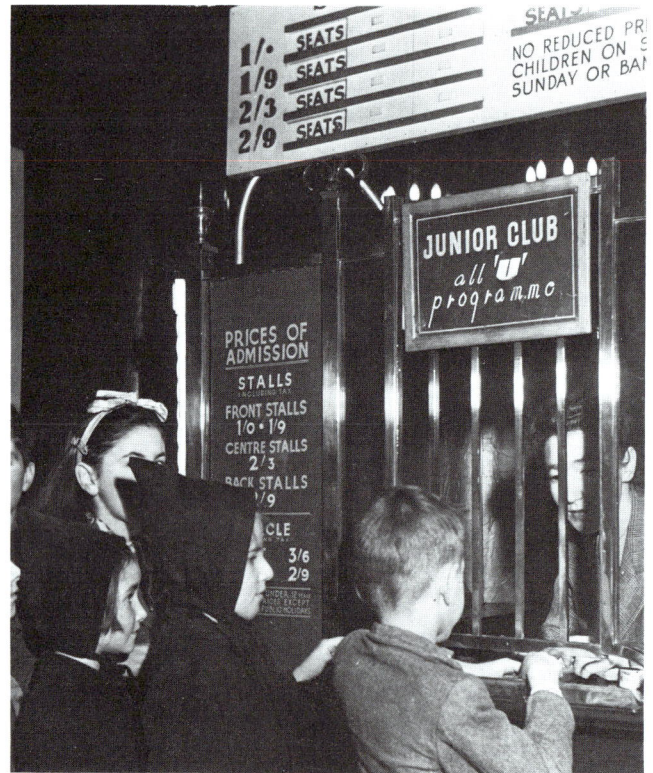

SEATS 1/-
SEATS 1/9
SEATS 2/3
SEATS 2/9

NO REDUCED PRI
CHILDREN ON
SUNDAY OR BAN

JUNIOR CLUB
all 'u'
programme

PRICES OF
ADMISSION
STALLS
FRONT STALLS
1/0 · 1/9
CENTRE STALLS
2/3
BACK STALLS
1/9

3/6
2/9

## Silent Movies

The first film was shown in a London theatre in 1896. It was put on between stage acts. Later special buildings, called cinemas, were built to show films.

At first films were silent. What the actors said came up as words on the screen, while a pianist in the cinema played music to suit the story.

## The Talkies

By the 1930s films had sound tracks. Talking and musical films became popular.

Tickets were cheap and cinemas were warm and comfortable. Sometimes there was an organist to entertain people during the interval.

## The Cinema in Wartime

In Book 1 you learned about the bombing of London and other large cities during the Second World War.

People inside a cinema could not hear the siren warning them of an air raid, so a notice like the one on the right was shown on the screen.

AN AIR RAID WARNING
HAS JUST BEEN SOUNDED

IF YOU WISH TO LEAVE THE CINEMA
PLEASE DO SO AS QUIETLY AS POSSIBLE.
THOSE WHO WISH TO REMAIN MAY DO SO
AT THEIR OWN RISK.

THE FILM NOW CONTINUES

Ask older folk what they did when the notice was put on the screen.

One woman remembers. "Few moved, I can tell you. Watching Clark Gable or Bing Crosby, who cared if a bomb dropped?"

Clark Gable

Bing Crosby

**A** People have always liked plays and play acting. Look at these three pictures and then answer the questions.

1. Two of the plays in the pictures are not performed by people. How are they performed?

2. What is the name of the show in the third picture? Have you ever seen one? If so, tell the story of what happened.

3. The second picture shows a pantomime. Is it Mother Goose, Dick Whittington, Puss in Boots or Cinderella? Tell the story of any pantomimes you have seen.

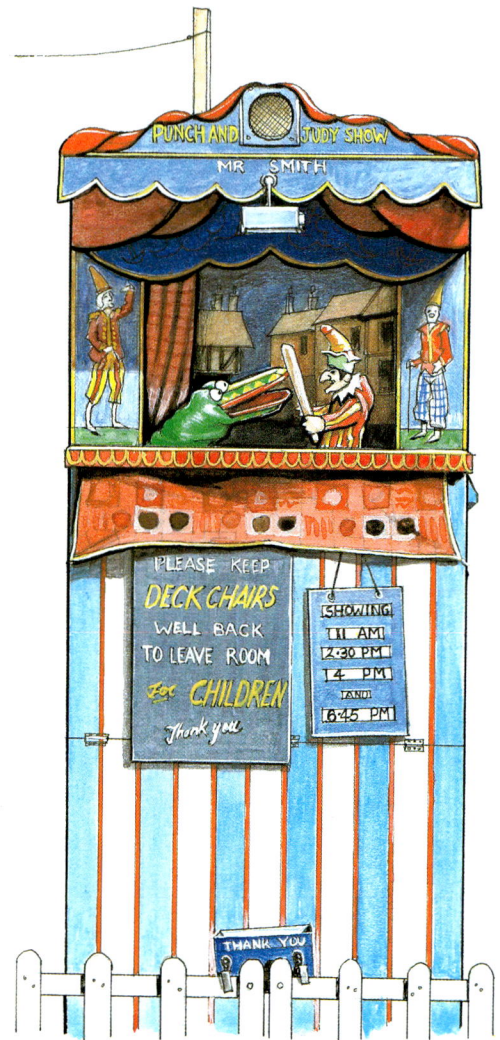

**B** Do you know who these famous film stars are? If not, ask some older people about them.

**C** Imagine you have been taken to the cinema for the first time in 1900. Write a letter to a friend telling him or her about it.

# Bobbies and Peelers

## Early Policemen

Have you ever thought why policemen are sometimes called "Bobbies"? It is because the first police force was formed in London by Sir Robert Peel.

Before that the only way to deal with a riot was to send for the army. Soldiers on horseback, armed with weapons, often killed or hurt people (as at the Peterloo Massacre, shown below).

Policemen carried one of these. It was called a truncheon. Why do you think this one has "V.R." painted on it? (If you want a clue, remember Unit 5.)

An early policeman would use the rattle below if he wanted other policemen to come and help him. How do policemen call for help today?

Sir Robert's "Peelers" carried no swords or pistols. They were dressed like this.

57

# Policemen in Brighton

Peel's police force was so successful that other towns copied the idea. In Brighton, Sussex, for example, thirty men were made policemen in 1838. Their pay was 90p a week and they had no holidays. They were given boots which were shapeless and could be worn on either foot.

How have the Brighton (now Sussex) police uniforms changed over the years? What differences do you see between the uniforms?

Brighton Police uniforms in (from left to right): 1880, 1930, 1930, 1885, 1939, 1841 and 1880.

An old police station. Policemen have stations just as soldiers have barracks or camps. They do not live in them but report to the station when they go on duty. Sometimes ordinary houses are used as police stations.

Brighton Police used a hand ambulance like this one until 1910. Why would police not do such a job today?

58

**Heavy raid last night**

**Mrs Pankhurst arrested outside Buckingham Palace**

**A** Old newspapers tell us a lot about the past. Here are two headlines and pictures. Say how the police would be involved each time.

**B** Here are pictures showing three ways in which people used to be punished. Find out more about them. What other kinds of old punishments have you heard of?

# Quiz

1. Why were many more houses needed in towns in Britain over one hundred years ago?

2. How did people heat their houses in 1850?

3. Why was the old Croydon Town Hall knocked down in the 1890s?

4. Who was the ruler of France during the long wars against Britain between 1804 and 1815?

5. What was the name of the famous English admiral killed at the Battle of Trafalgar in 1805?

6. Who was Prince Albert married to?

7. Which British Queen celebrated her jubilee in 1897?

8. What does the Latin word "Rex" mean?

9. What is the name of the city where a famous dog called "Bobby" lived?

10. What is another name for the South African War?

11. What famous English seaman sailed his ship around the world?

12. What did Mrs. Emmeline Pankhurst fight for?

13. Which English King had a White Swan as his badge?

14. What was the badge of King Edward III?

15. What English city has a badge with an ox on it?

16. What was a "moot"?

17. Why is the Arsenal Football team nicknamed "The Gunners"?

18. When were rules for playing football first made?

19. What game did William Ellis help to start?

20. Which two university crews row in the Boat Race each year?

21. Why did the Church provide schools for poor children?

22. What was a school log book?

23. What is a department store?

24. Why are places where things are made called "workshops"?

25. Which British store at first sold nothing costing more than 6d (old money)?

26. What is a mayor's "chain of office"?

27. What did the Saxon word "moot" mean?

28. Who were the two brothers who started a "Holy Club" when they were at University?

29. How did the Society of Friends get the nickname "Quakers"?

30. Who founded the Boy Scouts?

31. What year was the Festival of Britain held?

32. Who was Andrew Carnegie?

33. Why is Poppy Day in November?

34. Where is the Cenotaph?

35. What does the "Unknown Warrior" represent?

36. What was a Hurricane and when was it used?

37. Why is a senior nurse called "Sister"?

38. How did "Aunt Agatha's" newspaper column help people in East Grinstead?

39. Who were the "Guinea Pigs" in Queen Victoria Hospital, East Grinstead?

40. What did Henri Dunant help to found?

41. What did children see at a "Saturday Club" in 1948?

42. Who was Clark Gable?

43. Why were policemen at first called "Peelers"?

44. How many men were made policemen at Brighton, Sussex, in 1838?

45. What is a truncheon?

# Glossary

*(The number gives the unit where the words first appear)*

| | | Unit |
|---|---|---|
| **Advertisements** | different ways of telling people about goods for sale or an event like a play or a concert | 1 |
| **Armada** | a fleet of ships | 5 |
| **Captured** | a town, person or thing which has been taken prisoner | 3 |
| **Cellars** | rooms below ground level | 2 |
| **Certificate** | a document stating a person's qualifications, usually as a result of passing a test or examination | 8 |
| **Chimneys** | hollow stone or brick pillars to carry smoke and fumes out of houses | 1 |
| **Cipher** | initials of a person or company | 5 |
| **Commemorate** | to remember somebody or some event in a special way | 5 |
| **Factories** | large workshops making lots of goods | 2 |
| **Gadgets** | small fittings or pieces of machinery | 2 |
| **Grating** | small metal door for closing and opening, often has small holes in it to let in air | 2 |
| **Guildhalls** | another name for town halls | 4 |
| **Jubilee** | anniversary celebrations for 25, 50 ot 60 years of a reign or marriage | 5 |
| **Jugglers** | people who can throw and catch several objects at the same time | 9 |
| **Legends** | stories about earlier times which some people may believe to be true | 6 |
| **Mayor** | head of a town council | 10 |
| **Memorial** | statue or other monument in memory of a famous person | 1 |
| **Modern** | up to date | 2 |
| **Museum** | building to store and display objects from the past | 9 |
| **Organisation** | a group of people working together towards a special purpose | 10 |
| **Pantomime** | Christmas show usually telling a well known folk story, like "Jack and the Beanstalk" | 13 |

| | | |
|---|---|---|
| **Plaque** | tablet of metal or stone to commemorate some person or event | 5 |
| **Public Transport** | vehicles used to take people or things from one place to another on payment of a fare | 3 |
| **Shambles** | a place where butchers kill animals; also a mess or muddle | 4 |
| **Shepherd** | a person who looks after sheep | 5 |
| **Siege** | surrounding a place with soldiers to force the defenders to surrender | 4 |
| **Stadium** | fenced off field used for sporting events; from a Greek word | 7 |
| **Standard** | special flag showing badge of a family | 6 |
| **Surgeon** | person who carries out operations in hospital | 12 |
| **Temples** | buildings used for worship | 12 |
| **Thatched** | covered with a roof made of reeds | 2 |
| **Universities** | places of education for grown-up students | 7 |

# Index